Lancas
Cricketing Greats

57 of the best cricketers for Lancashire, 1864-1989

by Dean Hayes

Carnegie Press, 1989

Lancashire Cricketing Greats
by Dean P. Hayes

Typeset in 10pt Caslon and published by
Carnegie Press, 125 Woodplumpton Road,
Fulwood, Preston PR2 2LS. Tel (0772) 728868

Printed by Mather Brothers, 1 Garstang Road, Preston

ISBN 0 948789 33 6

The publishers would like to express their thanks to Lancashire County Cricket Club, in particular Malcolm
Lorimar, for their help in the preparation of this book for publication.

Contents

Foreword, by Clive Lloyd

AS AN ADOPTED Lancastrian, I feel quite honoured to be asked to write the foreword for this book, *Lancashire Cricketing Greats*.

Lancashire County Cricket Club was formed 125 years ago and, when I think of the galaxy of stars that treaded the hallowed turf of Old Trafford for Lancashire, I feel quite ecstatic that I am being mentioned along with players such as Ernest and John Tyldesley, Sydney Barnes, Robert Berry, Johnny Briggs, George Duckworth, Charlie Hallows, Len Hopwood, Albert Hornby, Jack Ikin, Winston Place, Archie MacLaren, Harry Makepeace, Cecil Parkin, Dick Pollard, Cyril Washbrook, and those of my own era – Brian Statham, Ken Higgs, Peter Lever, Ken Shuttleworth, Farokh Engineer, David Lloyd, Barry Wood, Jack Bond, David Hughes, Frank Hayes and the man who I thought was one of the best players in England but who never got the chance to represent his beloved country, the one and only Harry Pilling. I will always treasure those moment batting with Harry.

When I think of the halcyon days at Old Trafford during the late 1960s and the '70s, I will always hold dear the warmth of the people. They made me feel a true Lancastrian. Every time I walked to the wicket I felt that if I did not perform satisfactorily I would be disappointing quite a lot of people. They gave me an inner strength that made me want the reduce the opposition to mere minnions.

Lancashire will always be special to me, because I learnt quite a lot playing for this great Cricket Club, in my salad days, and I hope that I was able to repay them tenfold.

I will end with this quotation to the Lancashire Greats from 'A Psalm of Life'. "Lives of great men all remind us, we can make our lives sublime and departing leave behind us, footprints on the sands of time".

I am positive that this book should be in the home of every cricket lover and I am sure that the information in will be of great interest to everyone in Lancashire.

Introduction

LANCASHIRE COUNTY CRICKET CLUB was formed 125 years ago, in 1864, an extension of the Manchester Club which had already been playing at the present Old Trafford ground for seven years.

Lancashire cricket at the turn of the century must have been a wonderful sight. Crowds turned up in plenty. One Saturday in 1878, when Gloucestershire were the opponents and W. G. Grace was in their ranks, the crowd topped 17,000, people arriving on horseback, in carriages, by train or on foot.

Two of Lancashire's cricketing 'greats' in those early years were Hornby and Barlow. They have been given everlasting life in a beautiful poem by Francis Thompson. It is called *At Lords'*.

> *It is little I repair to the matches of the Southron folk*
> *Though my own red roses there may blow*
> *It is little I repair to the matches of the Southron folk*
> *Though the red roses crest the caps I know*
> *For the field is full of shades as I near the shadowy coast*
> *And a ghostly batsman plays to the bowling of a ghost*
> *And I look through my tears on a soundless-clapping host*
> *As the run-stealers flicker to and fro*
> *To and fro –*
> *O my Hornby and my Barlow long ago!*

Hornby first played for Lancashire in 1867 and was perhaps the more famous of this dynamic duo. Hornby and Barlow were the opening batsmen in 1881 when Lancashire won the County Championship for the first time. They went through a thirteen-match campaign unbeaten, with ten wins and three draws. Hornby was captain and had welded the County side into a tremendous cricketing force. Whilst he and Barlow were the mainstay of the batting, Alec Watson was one of the principal men who mattered with the ball. Along with Vernon Royle patrolling cover-point, it is quite understandable why Lancashire were so successful a team.

Not long after, a left-handed spinner by the name of Johnny Briggs was making great strides. He is the only cricketer who has scored 10,000 runs and taken 1,000 wickets for Lancashire. He is also the only cricketer who has scored a century and taken a 'hat-trick' in England *v.* Australia matches.

A few years later, two other 'greats' were beginning to get a mention in Lancashire cricketing circles. Albert Ward, who had initially played for Yorkshire before joining Lancashire, scoring runs as though they were going out of fashion. Arthur Mold came from Northamptonshire and, despite a suspect action, took wickets at a better rate than anyone yet who has worn the Red Rose.

In 1895, Lancashire scored her highest innings total, 801 against Somerset. A batsman by the name of Archie MacLaren scored 424 out of that total. He stands high among the great Lancashire players. MacLaren captained Lancashire in her next outright Championship victory, in 1904. He continued to play for the County until the outbreak of the First World War, when he was 43 years old. He hadn't quite finished yet, however; in fact, he ended on a high note – his last first-class innings was played for the M.C.C. against New Zealand in Wellington – when his score was 200 not out, at the age of 51!

MacLaren's cause was helped by having the likes of Sharp, Spooner and J.T. Tyldesley to bolster the batting, and Cuttell the bowling.

From 1899 until 1903, Lancashire had the services of that great bowler, Sydney Barnes. Whilst he did not always perform at his best for Lancashire, I feel that he richly deserces inclusion in a book about 'greats'. In those early years of the twentieth century, Lancashire was fortunate in having players rich in talent, Walter Brearley and Harry Dean being the pick of the bunch.

Despite all these great names, Lancashire had to wait a further twenty-two years before listing the County Championship again. In the 1920s, Lancashire developed a team which was undoubtedly the best ever to wear the Red-Rose. The team won the Championship outright in 1926, 1927, 1928 and 1930, and was second in 1929.

The greatest 'diddler' of them all, Cecil Parkin, had called it a day in 1926, the first year of Lancashire's winning streak. Harry Makepeace, a formidable man whose batting was primarily defensive, helped to provide the basis for a sound start in three of those seasons. Yet six 'greats' who were internationals formed the backbone of all four Championship winning teams. They were Ernest Tyldesley, Charlie Hallows, Dick Tyldesley, Jack Iddon, George Duckworth and Ted McDonald. Add to those the talents of Frank Watson, who was unlucky not to be capped by England, and you will realise that consistency was the name of the game.

In the four winning seasons, Australian McDonald took 623 wickets and was instrumental in providing victories for Lancashire, when matches looked to be heading for a draw. In 1929, when Lancashire finished second, McDonald (142) and Dick Tyldesley (154) took almost 300 wickets between them!

Perhaps 1928 was the most outstanding year. Lancashire did not lose a single match and Charlie Hallows scored 1,000 runs in May – only W. G. Grace and Wally Hammond also having achieved this feat. Lancashire took the title again in 1934, when players such as Len Hopwood, Eddie Paynter, Dick Pollard and a young Cyril Washbrook, added to the already talented Red-Rose side.

In 1935, the year after Lancashire won the Championship, George Duckworth gave way to the younger Farrimond. He was able to feel his way as a wicket-keeper and was also a player who could score runs. There was one comforting thought running through Old Trafford in the late thirties: players such as Washbrook, Paynter, Place, Pollard and Ikin were still on the threshold of their careers; the quality of Paynter's and Wahbrook's batting, in particular, shone through. Unfortunately, five long years of war was destined to turn the world – and Lancashire cricket – upside down.

When play resumed after the war, there was talk of Jack Iddon turning amateur to take charge at Old Trafford but, tragically, he was killed in a road accident just a few weeks before the 1946 season opened. Washbrook, Place and Pollard formed the nucleus of the re-formed team after the war and they were joined in1946 by newcomers Malcolm Hilton, Nigel Howard and Alan Wharton. The following two years saw the captaincy change hands to Ken Cranston. Place and Washbrook were still giving the County many three-figure starts and were far and away the best opening pair in county cricket.

At the end of 1948, Cranston announced his intention of concentrating on his dentistry practice in Liverpool and the captaincy was given to Nigel Howard. Whilst it was a difficult time for the young captain, he did insist on the introduction of several youngsters, Bob Berry, Brain Statham and Roy Tattersall, the latter two destined to make a great impact on the game.

In 1949, a new Australian recruit by the name of Ken Grieves joined Lancashire and was one of give Lancashire batsmen to top 1,000 runs that season. Howard became handicapped by illness and Lancashire didn't hesitate to ask Cyril Washbrook to take over. His bowlers gave him excellent support, both Statham and Thattersall took more than a hundred wickets and Hilton wasn't far behind. Howard resumed the captaincy again in 1953 but took the disappointing decision to retire at the end of that season.

In the 1950s, there arrived a crop of very talented youngsters, Tommy Greenhough bowling leg-breaks, Bob Barber, a schoolboy all-rounder and a promising opener by the name of Geoff Pullar. In 1955, a middle-order batsman gave much encouragement for the future – his name . . . Jack Bond. The long search for a worthwhile opening partner for Statham was solved in 1958, when Ken Higgs arrived from the Potteries to give England's premier strike bowler the support he had needed for so long.

In the early sixties, Bob Barber was allowed to move to Warwickshire, where he blossomed into a highly entertaining cricketer. Ken Grieves was made captain in 1963 and again the following year, the club's centenary year. He introduced little Harry Pilling to bolster the batting and, with Peter Lever batting well, these were two other players who made regular appearances. In 1965, Lancashire's greatest bowler, Brian Statham, was appointed captain. Newcomer Ken Shuttleworth was bowling well and yet another acquisition from Yorkshire, Barry Wood, arrived on the scene, as did David Lloyd, an all-rounder who was to prove in the years ahead what a talented player he was.

The next years were successful ones for the County in terms of one-day cricket. Jack Bond was made captain and the County secured the services of two superb overseas players, Farokh Engineer and Clive Lloyd. Lloyd, in particular, was one of the most attractive stroke players in the game. The John Player League and Gillette Cup trophies seemed permanent fixtures in the Old Trafford trophy room. Two other one-day specialists were also joining Lancashire in the late sixties, David Hughes and Jack Simmons. More than twenty years on, they are both still performing for the Red-Rose.

The 1970s saw the emergence of Frank Hayes as perhaps England's 'Great White Hope'. Whilst performing for Lancashire, he did not perform as well at test level, apart, ironically, from his first international test. Towards the end of the decade, Paul Allott arrived on the scene and progressed well to play at international level.

There has been no shortage of 'great' players since the Second World War, with Cyril Washbrook, Brian Statham and Clive Lloyd pre-eminent.

The years ahead seem bright and, if I were writing this book in a few years' time, then players such as Neil Fairbrother, Wasim Akram, Philip de Freitas and Michael Atherton would undoubtedly be included.

We all have our heroes, but the rich character and humour of these Lancashire cricketing greats is there for all to see . . .

Paul Allott

Birthplace:	Altrincham
Born:	14th September 1956
Died:	—
Played:	1978 –

Averages in all first-class Lancashire matches

Matches	Innings	Not Outs	Runs	Highest Score	Average	100s	50s
165	183	42	2,480	88	17.58	—	7

Runs	Wickets	Average	Best	5 Wickets	10 Wickets
11,079	475	23.32	8–48	19	—

Number of Test Appearances – 13

PAUL ALLOTT attended Altrincham Grammar School, where his talent was recognised and where he was considered as a player for the future. From school, he moved into the England Schools Cricket Association Under-19 side, bowling 'big in-swingers'. He toured the West Indies in 1976 with the young side which included David Gower and Mike Gatting. This was the year that he represented Cheshire in the Minor Counties, followed a year later by his Lancashire 2nd XI debut.

Paul attended Durham University, where he obtained a teaching certificate, with Geography as his main subject. Fellow Lancashire players, Graeme Fowler and Gehan Mendis were also studying there, and it is little wonder that they won the U.A.U. Championship.

Paul Allott was really born into one-day cricket – his first match for Lancashire was in the Benson and Hedges Cup, his second in the John Player League. Allott soon realised the importance of line and length and added an ever increasing pace and movement off the seam to his repertoire.

He went out to Tasmania with Jack Simmons and, on the slow wickets, he was forced to concentrate all the more on line and length. He was in the same Lancashire XI when Michael Holding made his county debut against Gloucestershire. Allott took 8–48 and said at the time: "Batsmen obviously aren't going to take chances against him, so they'll take chances against me" – a typically modest approach from a man who is quiet, reserved and softly spoken off the field, but ready to fight on it!

Standing around 6 feet 4 inches high, this fair-haired bowler is strongly built. He is a right-arm fast-meduim bowler with a high action. He is also a more than useful batsman, possessing a sound temperament. He has represented England on thirteen occasions. On his Test debut against Australia in 1981, Paul showed all these important qualities, hitting an undefeated 52 and taking 4 for 48.

Unfortunately, injuries have deprived him from making more international appearances, especially at home, where I feel that he would have been very successful. The Lancashire Committee have granted Paul a well deserved benefit next year, 1990.

Bob Barber

Birthplace:	Manchester
Born:	26th September 1935
Died:	—
Played:	1954-1962

Averages in all first-class Lancashire matches

Matches	Innings	Not Outs	Runs	Highest Score	Average	100s	50s
155	264	25	6,760	175	28.28	7	29

Runs	Wickets	Average	Best	5 Wickets	10 Wickets
4,768	152	31.36	7–35	3	—

Number of Test Appearances – 28

BOB BARBER had been a schoolboy prodigy. At Ruthin School, he did the 'double' – 1,000 runs and 100 wickets. He even played in three matches for Lancashire while he was still at school!

Bob Barber seems to have had dificulty choosing whether to play right- or left-handed – he was an attacking left-handed batsman with a superb array of shots all around the wicket and a very talented leg-break bowler, but right-handed! Add to this his excellence in the field, notably in the leg-trap and you have a superb all-round cricketer.

In 1960, at the age of twenty-four, he was appointed captain of Lancashire and, in the same year, won his first England cap. As a captain, he was often criticised for not bowling himself enough – this showed a great deal of unselfishness, explained in part by the fact that Tommy Greehough, a rival leg-spinner who was hoping to gain international honours, was also in the side.

There is no doubt about it, Barber was an individualist. He conformed to no pattern and was seen by some as unorthodox, with a mind and a temperament all his own.

In the second Test of the 1964-65 South African tour (after Barber had moved on to pastures new) he had made 97 out of the first 146. His partner at this time was the new England cricketing supremo, Ted Dexter. Though within a fraction of his century, Barber went up to Dexter and said "Right – six or out!". "Don't be so bloody stupid", said Dexter. But Barber said, "I mean it". Off-spinner Seymour was bowling at the time. Barber advanced to hit him straight, allowed for the spin which wasn't there and deflected the delivery into his wicket. He was not disappointed that he hadn't reached a ton. He gambled and lost!

Barber was an unselfish cricketer. For all his individualism, he always put the team first.

His outspokenness did not always please the Lancashire Committee and, after two years, he was relieved of the captaincy, the official reason being that the responsibility was handicapping his development as an international player. Eventually, he moved on to Warwickshire and it was at Edgbaston that Barber's best form emerged – more the pity for Lancashire.

Barber was an adventurous cricketer and even after retirement the spirit is still there. He took part in an arduous expedition in the Himalayan mountains.

Richard Barlow

Birthplace:	Bolton		
Born:	28th May 1851		
Died:	31st July 1919		
Played:	1871-1891		

Averages in all first-class Lancashire matches

Matches	Innings	Not Outs	Runs	Highest Score	Average	100s	50s
249	426	45	7,765	117	20.38	2	29

Runs	Wickets	Average	Best	5 Wickets	10 Wickets
10,010	736	13.60	9–39	55	12

Number of Test Appearances – 17

RICHARD GORTON BARLOW was born in 1851 at Barrow Bridge, Bolton. He had to make his early cricketing opportunities for himself – he used to play truant from school in order to practise with a bat hewn from a chunk of wood and a ball pieced together with cloth and string!

As a boy, he had batted and bowled left-handed but, on the advice of his father, he began to bat right-handed – in an aim, apparently, to avoid the supposed awkward appearance of batting left-handed. He used mainly the forward defensive stroke and acquired the reputation of a stone-waller.

He was a very cautious batsman, but never negative. He scored more than 7,000 runs for Lancashire at a time when few first-class matches were played. Perhaps eleven players like Barlow would prove tedious to say the least, but one such player is of tremendous value to a team. Many times, Barlow saved both Lancashire and England by his resolute defence. Twelve times he carried his bat through an innings and on many other occasions his was the last wicket to fall.

Barlow kept himself very trim, in peak condition – no day in the field was ever too long for him.

Barlow was also a useful bowler, bowling left-handed. He was nearer medium-paced than slow, spinning the ball away from the bat and the left-hander's ball which goes with the arm. It was said that he reserved a special ball for W. G. and, certainly, no one in that particular era was more successful

in dismissing the great man cheaply than Richard Barlow.

It was generally thought that Barlow's finest innings was played at Trent Bridge for the North of England against the visiting Australians in 1884. The North were dismissed for 91 (Barlow 10 not out) in the first innings. Spofforth, who had bowled extremely well in that innings, was confident that the North wouldn't get anywhere near even that total in their second innings. When the North had tumbled to 53 for 5, it looked as though Spofforth's prediction would come true. Flowers joined Barlow and they put on 158 for the sixth wicket. Barlow was last out, for 101. His performance with the bat was equalled by his feat with the ball, taking 10 for 45 in the match.

Barlow is the only cricketer to be picked for England with the specific intention that he should open both the batting and the bowling. He toured Australia on three occasions, not missing a single game! On a crumbling Old Trafford wicket, his stone-walling technique pulled England through the game against the Aussies. He backed up this resolute display with bowling figures of 7–44 in Australia's second innings.

Barlow holds two records. He is the only player to open both batting and bowling for his country and he is the only Lancashire player to top the county's batting and bowling averages in the same season, that of 1882. Barlow was also one of the few first-class batsmen never to 'bag a pair'.

Barlow's sporting prowess did not end there. He was a competent goalkeeper and also a soccer referee. He was in charge of the famous cup-tie when Preston North End defeated Hyde United 26–0. Barlow was also so successful as a track sprinter that he was offered on numerous occasions to make it his profession.

He also fancied himself as an inventor. In 1890 when the Old Trafford Test was rained off without a ball being bowled, he suggested that the disappointment could have been avoided if his patent wicket-protector had been purchased and used!

On his retirement from first-class cricket, he became a Test Match umpire and a good one at that! He also moved to the coast at Lytham where every part of his home was a cricket museum. There was a crest over the front door, a stained glass window in the vestibule with Barlow himself as the central figure; tiles on the fireplace had cricket pictures in them and cricket bats were even hung on the wall of his bathroom!

Unfortunately, Barlow's marriage did not last long and this quiet, unassuming man was left to live his life alone among his trophies and memories.

Sydney Barnes

Birthplace:	Smethwick
Born:	19th April 1873
Died:	26th December 1967
Played:	1899–1903

Averages in all first-class Lancashire matches

Matches	Innings	Not Outs	Runs	Highest Score	Average	100s	50s
46	58	20	452	35	11.89	—	—

Runs	Wickets	Average	Best	5 Wickets	10 Wickets
4,459	225	19.81	8–37	19	4

Number of Test Appearances – 27

AFTER STARTING his cricketing career with mediocre performances for Warwickshire, Barnes served as a professional in the Lancashire League. He was invited for trials to the nets at Old Trafford and to play in the last match of the 1901 season. He had played in two games in 1899 with only moderate success. He was professional at Burnley and his appearance in that last match against Leicestershire when he took 6–70 proved to be an event of great importance for English cricket. He impressed Archie MacLaren and was invited to tour Down Under with his team.

His inclusion was a great surprise to many, and even though he had to withdraw half-way through the tour, he had already done enough to establish his reputation.

Many people who both watched and played with Sydney Francis Barnes, claimed he was the best bowler ever. He was a right-arm medium fast bowler artd could make devastating use of the seam and shine of a new ball and swing and cut the ball when it was old.

On his return from Australia, he was persuaded to play on a more regular basis for Lancashire and did so, but only for two seasons!

Barnes had no real taste for everyday cricket. He was not a man who could toil all day for very little reward and then come back the following day for more.

Unfortunately, relations at Old Trafford became sour and Barnes was forced to return to League Cricket with Lancashire the ones to suffer.

He is probably the greatest bowler who has ever appeared for the Red-Rose county, but his greatness doesn't belong to those days!

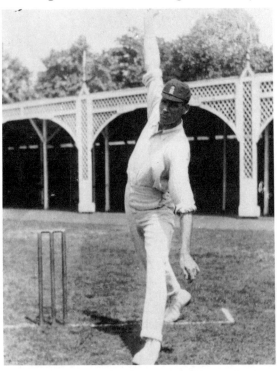

Robert Berry

Birthplace:	Manchester
Born:	29th January 1926
Died:	—
Played:	1948–1954

Averages in all first-class Lancashire matches

Matches	Innings	Not Outs	Runs	Highest Score	Average	100s	50s
93	85	34	427	27*	8.37	—	—

Runs	Wickets	Average	Best	5 Wickets	10 Wickets
5,900	259	22.77	10–102	13	2

Number of Test Appearances – 2

BOB BERRY began his cricketing career in the Lancashire and Cheshire League. He was an orthodox left-arm spin bowler, but during his years at Old Trafford, he had to fight for his place in the county first team with other spinners.

He was a much better bowler than his figures suggest, though he did one take ten wickets in an innings.

Berry became tired of having to fight for a place in the county first team which he regarded as his and so he moved on to end his career with Derbyshire and Worcestershire. Lancashire's loss was their gain!

Jack Bond

Birthplace:	Kearsley	
Born:	6th May 1932	
Died:	—	
Played:	1955–1972	

Averages in all first-class Lancashire matches

Matches	Innings	Not Outs	Runs	Highest Score	Average	100s	50s
344	522	76	11,867	157	22.60	14	53

Runs	Wickets	Average	Best	5 Wickets	10 Wickets
69	0	—	—	—	—

Number of Test Appearances – 0

JACK BOND was born at Kearsley near Bolton and was educated at Bolton School. Much of his early cricket was played in the Bolton League.

Bond made his debut for Lancashire against Surrey at Old Trafford towards the end of the 1955 season – failing to score in his first innings! It took a few years for Bond to really arrive. In 1961, he scored 1,701 runs, including a superb century in only 93 minutes against Sussex at Old Trafford and was consequently awarded his county cap. The following year, he reached his peak. He topped 2,000 runs, including five centuries.

In 1963, just as it seemed international honours would come his way, one ball from West Indian paceman Wes Hall set him back. The ball from Hall broke his wrist and Bond never (in terms of figures) reproduced the sparkle he'd shown in 1961 and 1962. In fact, halfway through the 1964 season, he lost his first team place.

Lancashire lost faith in this tough uncompromising batsman. Yet there is no doubt in my mind that Lancashire needed his ability and graft. When Bond did regain his first team place, he was once again dropped midway through the season and this was the case in 1965, 1966 and 1967. There was great speculation that Bond's days at Old Trafford were numbered and that he wouldn't be retained. In 1965, when Jack wasn't required for first-team duty, he played as a stand-in professional in the Bolton Association, but typical of the man, he didn't take a fee.

Yet, in 1968, Lancashire somewhat reluctantly it must be said, turned to Bond as captain. Bond was always a team man, unselfish in his approach to life. This I'm sure was instrumental in Bond assembling such a capable side in those heady years, not too long ago! Bond was popular with his fellow players, and respected too. Since he himself had endured failure, he tolerated it in others. When Bond took over the captaincy, he said "We are going to enjoy our cricket" – and the Lancashire team took their orders to heart. Success followed with John Player League and Gillette Cup titles coming with regularity.

Tactically, there were few Lancashire captains to match him. The fielders were kept on their toes as Bond changed the field to suit batsmen and mood.

Bond played the game with a keen sense of humour. Thousands of television viewers who witnessed a Sunday League fixture at Buxton against Derbyshire, must have doubled up in laughter as Bond up-rooted a stump and holding it like a spear, proceeded to pursue a dog that had lost its master.

In 1972, after leading Lancashire to their third successive Gillette Cup Final victory, he announced his retirement and was appointed to the coaching staff. His initial stay was short, departing to take over the captaincy at Nottinghamshire. After a spell as a Test Selector, he took up the position as coach/groundsman at the King William College Castletown on the Isle of Man. He then accepted an offer to return to Old Trafford as team manager, sadly departing a few years ago.

Off the field, Jack Bond liked nothing better than to listen to the sound of brass bands, but in recent times, he has spent much more time on the golf course. On the field, he was recognised throughout the first-class game as a shrewd skipper, always leading by example. He played a great part in the resurgence of Lancashire cricket in the late 1960s and early 1970s.

Walter Brearley

Birthplace:	Bolton
Born:	11th March 1876
Died:	13th January 1937
Played:	1902–1911

Averages in all first-class Lancashire matches

Matches	Innings	Not Outs	Runs	Highest Score	Average	100s	50s
106	145	23	749	38	6.13	—	—

Runs	Wickets	Average	Best	5 Wickets	10 Wickets
12,907	690	18.70	9–47	79	24

Number of Test Appearances – 4

WALTER BREARLEY didn't play first-class cricket until he was 26 years old, though he had played a great deal of club cricket with both Bolton and Manchester, gaining a reputation as a fast bowler.

He made his county debut in 1902 against Sussex at Brighton, but his start was a modest one. The following season saw him play fifteen games and take 69 wickets at a cost of 23 runs each. It was in 1904, however, that Walter Brearley came into his own and, largely as a result of his efforts, Lancashire won the County Championship. He ended the season with 95 wickets (this would have been more if he hadn't been injured in August) and was considered the best amateur fast bowler in England.

It was at the end of this season that Brearley's first argument with authority arose. He was left out of the Rest of England v Champion County game and promptly announced his retirement from the first-class game. Happily, everything was resolved and Brearley was there to start the next season.

1905 must surely have been Brearley's greatest season. He took 133 wickets at 19 runs each for Lancashire (181 in all matches).

His greatest game must surely have been against Somerset. He had figures of 17–137. In Somerset's first innings he took 9–47 and 8–90 in their second, including four wickets in four balls. When the Australians visited Old Trafford, he bowled with great fire and passion and took 7–115.

His success that season led inevitably to his first test appearance. He played in the last two Tests that summer at Old Trafford and the Oval. He couldn't have felt homesick, as he was joined for these two matches by MacLaren, Spooner and J.T. Tyldesley. At Old Trafford, he took 4–72 and 4–54 to acquit himself extremely well. At the Oval, he bowled superbly to claim 5–110 in 31 overs.

Once again Brearley brushed with authority and tendered his resignation. He was back for the start of the season, but only played in five matches – Lancashire sorely missed his bowling. He only returned as a regular in 1908, taking 148 wickets in 17 Championship matches at 15 runs each. He was also chosen as one of Wisden's 'Five Cricketers of the Year'.

In 1909, Brearley took 118 wickets at 16 runs each and Lancashire finished

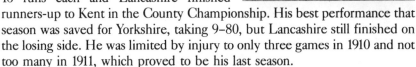

runners-up to Kent in the County Championship. His best performance that season was saved for Yorkshire, taking 9–80, but Lancashire still finished on the losing side. He was limited by injury to only three games in 1910 and not too many in 1911, which proved to be his last season.

No one 'enjoyed' the Roses matches more than Walter Brearley – he thrived on the big occasion. In 14 encounters with the 'White Rose' he took 125 wickets at a cost of only 16 runs each.

Going out to bat, Brearley would often vault the pavilion gate. He was not, however, implying that he would be out in the middle for a lengthy spell; quite the reverse, he very rarely troubled the scorers! Brearley's jumping feats were many, one of them being an ability to clear a full-sized billiard table!

Brearley's run was short, about eight paces, his great speed coming from his powerful shoulders and a full follow through. He could bring the ball back and make it go with his arm, but he believed the wickets were there to be hit, hence he was also very accurate. Whilst his deliveries looked the same, the balls in fact were delivered from different points of the crease. He didn't believe that any batsman could bat – "They're probably a lot of ruddy teetotallers anyway."

Walter Brearley was willing to bowl all day long. He never grumbled about hard work. In fact, I'm sure he'd have bowled at both ends if the rules had permitted this!

Johnny Briggs

	Birthplace:	Sutton-in-Ashfield
	Born:	3rd October 1862
	Died:	11th January 1902
	Played:	1879–1900

Averages in all first-class Lancashire matches

Matches	Innings	Not Outs	Runs	Highest Score	Average	100s	50s
391	602	39	10,707	186	19.01	9	43

Runs	Wickets	Average	Best	5 Wickets	10 Wickets
26,464	1,696	15.60	10–55	161	41

Number of Test Appearances – 33

JOHNNY BRIGGS was born in Nottinghamshire, but his family moved to Lancashire when he was a small boy. He first played for Lancashire at the age of 17, in 1879. He appears to have won his place in the county side initially for his fielding, for his batting and bowling figures were very mediocre.

However, he arrived at Old Trafford as a promising batsman and once he had settled down he showed incredible power and timing that would have secured him a place in most other county sides of that era.

He was asked to bowl more and more for Lancashire and this, coupled with a decrease in pace, were the main reasons for his successful development as a bowler. He was a left-arm bowler with a run-up that amounted to no more than a couple of paces. Each delivery was tempting to the batsman, but to contend with, there was length, flight, spin, changes of pace and in his early days a well disguised fast straight one. As C. B. Fry said of him "a professor of diddling, considered as one of the exact sciences".

He was a brilliant fielder to his own bowling and there was no-one in the game that got through an over as quick!

He was the idol of the Old Trafford crowds and his love of the game was equalled only by the enjoyment of the company of the men who played it. He would often stop on his way to the ground to play an impromptu game with local children – he possessed a childlike capacity for the enjoyment of simple things.

Johnny Briggs is the only Lancashire player to have taken over 1,000 wickets and scored more than 10,000 runs.

In 1885, just three days after his wedding, he hit his top score of 186 at Aigburth against the men of Surrey.

In 1888, he took 160 wickets and was included in Wisden's gallery of 'Six Great Bowlers'.

'Roses' matches always brought the best out of Johnny Briggs. In 1891 after bowling Yorkshire to defeat at Bradford, he took 6–76 and 8–46 in the

return game at Old Trafford. In the 1892 fixture at Old Trafford, Johnny Briggs had the sort of match one dreams about. He scored 115 in the Lancashire innings and followed it up with 8–113, bowling unchanged.

In 1893 at Headingley, Briggs took 8–19 as Lancashire won by an innings, yet the return fixture brought perhaps the closest finish to a 'Roses' match. Lancashire were dismissed for 64, but Yorkshire could only muster 58 in reply. In their second innings, Lancashire were shot out for 50, leaving Yorkshire just 57 to win. They started well, putting on 24 before the first wicket fell. Then wickets began to fall steadily, and as George Ulyett faced Briggs, the score stood at 51–9. A six would win it, Briggs tossed the ball up, Ulyett gave it a mighty clout, but there on the boundary waiting for the ball, were the safe hands of

Albert Ward. Lancashire had won and Johnny Briggs had taken 11–60. He played 33 times for England, all but two of the games being against Australia. He took 118 wickets at 17.74 and scored over 800 runs at an average of 18. In the two tests he played against South Africa, he took 6–73 in one test and 15–128 in the other.

Johnny Briggs is the only England player to have taken a 'hat-trick' and scored a hundred against Australia. In the 1899 test match at Headingley, he was attacked by epilepsy. He recovered sufficiently to play again the following year, taking his customary 100 wickets (including all ten wickets in an innings against Worcestershire).

Johnny Briggs suffered a relapse and was put in a mental home, where he died some two years later, at the age of 39. It was a very sad end for this best loved of all Lancashire cricketers.

Ken Cranston

Birthplace:	Aigburth
Born:	20th October 1917
Died:	—
Played:	1947–1948

Averages in all first-class Lancashire matches

Matches	Innings	Not Outs	Runs	Highest Score	Average	100s	50s
50	57	9	1,928	155*	40.16	2	14

Runs	Wickets	Average	Best	5 Wickets	10 Wickets
3,267	142	23.00	7–43	10	1

Number of Test Appearances – 8

KEN CRANSTON'S introduction into first-class cricket was unusual to say the least. He played his schoolboy cricket in Liverpool, where he attended the Liverpool College. He was a regular member of the first XI from 1930–1935. In 1934, he played for the Young Amateurs against the Young Professionals at Lord's and a year later, he secured a place in the Public Schools XI against the Army.

He went on to appear for the Royal Navy, Combined Services and Club Cricket Conference, but in 1947, he not only made his debut, but also became captain of Lancashire's first team. The game of cricket suffered greatly when at the end of the 1948 season, he called it a day, due to the claims of his dental practice.

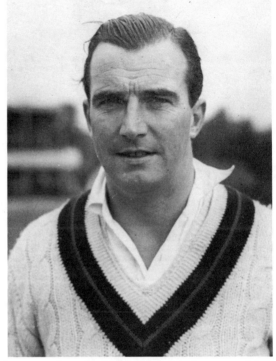

Ken Cranston's two years in the first-class game were, he reckons, the happiest of his life.

In 1947, he guided Lancashire to third place in the County Championship and to fifth place the following year. Also in 1947, he only just failed to complete the 'double' of 1,000 runs and 100 wickets.

Cranston hit two hundreds for Lancashire against Hampshire at Bournemouth and Warwickshire at Edgbaston. Yet if one were to ask Cranston to name his most memorable match, it was the county game against the Australians in which his role was negligible. This was the time Malcolm Hilton dismissed Don Bradman twice in two days.

Cranston was a very gifted all-rounder. He was a fast-medium opening bowler and a very forceful right-handed batsman. Despite only playing first-class cricket for two years, he went on to represent his country on eight occasions, including once as skipper against the West Indies. He scored 209 runs and took 18 wickets in his eight international matches.

Cranston's record for Lancashire in the two years he played was quite exceptional. He scored just short of 2,000 runs at an average of over 40 and took 142 wickets at a cost of 23 runs each. It was a sad day for Lancashire cricket when this amiable thirty year old went back to extracting teeth!

Willis Cuttell

Birthplace:	Sheffield
Born:	13th September 1864
Died:	9th December 1929
Played:	1896–1906

Averages in all first-class Lancashire matches

Matches	Innings	Not Outs	Runs	Highest Score	Average	100s	50s
213	294	30	5,389	137	20.41	5	18

Runs	Wickets	Average	Best	5 Wickets	10 Wickets
14,890	760	19.59	8–105	50	8

Number of Test Appearances – 2

WILLIS CUTTELL began his career with Yorkshire (we forgive him that little indiscretion!) before joining Lancashire.

Cuttell was a great surprise – playing regularly in first-class cricket for the

first time at thirty-three years of age. He immediately established himself as one of the best medium-paced bowlers in the country.

In 1898, he took 114 wickets and scored 1,003 runs, being the first Lancashire player to qualify for a place in the list of 'All-Round Cricketers'. Also in 1898, he went to South Africa with a team captained by Lord Hawke and did well as a bowler.

Cuttell really was a top-class all-rounder. He was a hard-hitting batsman who could also defend strongly. His highest score was 137 against Nottinghamshire in 1899 in a match played at Old Trafford. He could also bowl slow and turn the ball either way, but it was the ball which came from the leg with his arm which made him so effective. In 1897, Cuttell took 4 wickets for 8 runs against Sussex at Hove. In 1898, at Old Trafford against Gloucestershire he took 8–105. In 1901 at Derby he took 7–19 and three years later in 1904 at Old Trafford in the match against Kent, he took 4 wickets for 3 runs.

In 1907, the year after he left the first-class scene, he was appointed coach at Rugby School, where he stayed for some twenty years. He then acted as a first-class umpire for two seasons.

Harry Dean

Birthplace:	Burnley
Born:	13th August 1884
Died:	12th March 1957
Played:	1906–1921

Averages in all first-class Lancashire matches

Matches	Innings	Not Outs	Runs	Highest Score	Average	100s	50s
256	354	118	2,449	49*	10.37	—	—

Runs	Wickets	Average	Best	5 Wickets	10 Wickets
22,828	1,267	18.01	9–31	96	24

Number of Test Appearances – 3

HARRY DEAN came into the Lancashire side in 1906 and right from the start, was prepared to bowl his heart out for his side.

Dean was a left-arm swerve bowler, yet if the wicket suited, he could bowl left-arm spin – a more than useful bowler to have on your side! On no fewer than eight occasions did Dean take a hundred wickets or more in a season. In 1907, he took 110 wickets, including 9–46 against Derbyshire at Chesterfield. In 1909, he took 9–35 against Warwickshire at Aigburth. The following year, he destroyed Somerset at Bath. He took 9–77 in the first innings and 7–26 in the second – match figures of 16–103.

In 1911, a gloriously hot season, Dean got through more overs and took more wickets than any bowler in the country. His figures in that particular

season included 8–121 against Warwickshire and 9–109 against
Leicestershire. When Hampshire
visited Old Trafford that summer,
Lancashire scored 676 runs in only 6½
hours. Dean, with the help of Lol
Cook, dismissed Hampshire for 102
and 119. Lancashire won by an innings
and 455 runs, their biggest ever
recorded win and the third widest
victory margin in the history of the
County Championship.

In 1912 the wickets were much
softer, so Dean switched to spin rather
than his swerve and benefited greatly.
He took 136 wickets that season, his
best performance bringing match
figures of 15–108 against Kent at Old
Trafford. It was also in this season that
Harry Dean made his test debut. He
played in matches against Australia and
South Africa in the triangular
tournament. He took 4–19 against
Australia in the first 'timeless' test as
they were dismissed for just 65. At
Headingley, he had match figures of 5–56 against the South Africans.

The performance for which Harry Dean will always be remembered took
place in 1913. Lancashire had arranged an extra Roses match as part of the
celebrations in connection with King George V's visit to Liverpool.
Lancashire won the match played at Aigburth by three wickets. Dean had
match figures of 17 for 91.

Like many other Lancashire cricketing greats, seasons were taken from
him due to the war. It is possible that he may have challenged Johnny Briggs'
record of 1688 Lancashire wickets.

In 1919, he didn't have a successful season, his 51 wickets costing almost
30 runs a piece. The following season, he returned to something like his best,
taking 124 wickets, including 8–80 against Surrey at Old Trafford.

In 1921, whilst in indifferent form, he faded from the first-class game. He
had given everything to Lancashire, no other bowler has had a greater heart
than Harry Dean.

George Duckworth

Birthplace:	Warrington
Born:	9th May 1901
Died:	5th January 1966
Played:	1923–1938

Averages in all first-class Lancashire matches

Matches	Innings	Not Outs	Runs	Highest Score	Average	100s	50s
424	455	170	4,174	75	14.64	—	6

Caught	Stumped	Total
634	288	922

Number of Test Appearances – 24

GEORGE DUCKWORTH was born in Warrington and was educated at the local Grammar School. He first played for Lancashire in 1923 and kept the first team spot his own until his retirement from the first-class game in 1937. His total of 107 dismissals in 1928 is still a record for a Lancashire wicket-keeper in one season.

Between the years 1926–1930, he was at the peak of his career. Some of his takes down the leg-side standing back to Ted McDonald were I believe out of this world.

Throughout his career, he never lost his terrific zest for the game or his ebullient boyishness. Duckworth possessed a famous high-pitched appeal 'the cock's shrill clarion' – a vehement demand for justice. With

all his heart and mind, he would will the batsman out and if he thought success had come his way, all the pent-up feelings inside him found expression in one almighty cry.

If a wicket-keeper can be aggressive, then George Duckworth certainly was!

The influence of a great wicket-keeper on the fielding of the whole side is immense. Duckworth loved to have the ball hurled back at him at great speed, even when there was little chance of a run-out.

He toured Australia on three occasions, firstly in 1928–29 as the number one stumper and then in 1932–33 and 1936–37, when he was understudy to Les Ames of Kent.

When Duckworth toured Australia in 1928–29, M. A. Noble wrote of him:

> "He bustles along between overs as eager to continue the strife as a boy is to ride his first two-wheeler bicycle and his youthfulness and enthusiasm appeal to the crowd."

He did have his off-days. In 1930 at the Oval in the fifth test against Australia, he dropped Woodfull at 6, Ponsford at 23 and 45 and Bradman at 82. Woodfull ended with 54, Ponsford 110 and Sir Don 232. It was said that Duckworth cost England somewhere in the region of 285 runs and the opportunity of England winning or squaring the series.

On his retirement from first-class cricket, he became county scorer, and later a B.B.C. commentator and then baggage master for touring test teams. He possessed an abounding zest for anything he did – cricket quite obviously, but also Rugby League, carrier pigeons and Rupert Brooke's poetry!

He was certainly a real 'character' who added great flavour to the game.

Farokh Engineer

Birthplace:	Bombay, India	
Born:	25th February 1938	
Died:	—	
Played:	1968–1976	

Averages in all first-class Lancashire matches

Matches	Innings	Not Outs	Runs	Highest Score	Average	100s	50s
175	262	39	5,942	141	26.64	4	25

Runs	Wickets	Caught	Stumped	Total
10	0	429	35	464

Number of Test Appearances – 46 (India)

FAROKH ENGINEER was born in 1938 in Bombay, the son of Parsee parents. He made his first-class debut in 1958 in India and went on to make his test debut against England at Kanpur in the 1961–62 series. He toured England with the Indian squad in 1967 and a year later, he joined Lancashire on a special registration.

His first appearance was against Kent at Canterbury, but despite taking 62 victims, he had scored only 747 runs from 42 completed innings. The Lancashire supporters had expected a batsman wicket-keeper not a wicket-keeper batsman.

In 1969, he most certainly would have topped 1,000 runs but ended on 952, as he missed the last four games of the season. He hit his first Red-Rose century that year, 103 not out against Glamorgan at Swansea. He showed time and time again what a masterly batsman he could be, as he would take runs off all bowlers to all parts of all grounds.

I remember in 1969, attending a televised game at Southport. Glamorgan were the opponents and were dismissed for 112. Lancashire won by nine wickets, Engineer hitting 78 not out in flamboyant style. The Glamorgan opening bowler, Ossie Wheatley, was heard to say "I don't mind him charging, but I do wish he would let me set off first."

Engineer was a natural athlete with a magnificent eye both behind and in front of the stumps.

As a wicket-keeper he would often take many of his catches in front of first slip, leaping with great reflexes. A friendly man, he would often exchange words with the batsman – method in his madness?. It wasn't just the opposition batsmen he would talk to, but anybody! The topic of conversation wasn't always cricket. Engineer was adored by youngsters. I remember on many occasions, him practising before the start of a game and encouraging all the young lads to bowl and field to him. He was one of the few modern day wicket-keepers who would stand right up to the fast-medium bowlers.

Engineer has probably done more than any other player to promote Indian cricket to world-class status – certainly more than any other player since the war, and that includes Kapil Dev and Sunil Gavasker. He represented India on 46 occasions, scoring 2,611 runs at an average of 31.08; he also recorded 82 dismissals, 66 caught and 16 stumped.

He was a dashing player with a wide array of strokes. He was very exciting to watch and play was certainly never dull when he was around. When I watched Farokh, he would excite me one minute and infuriate me the next – but I wouldn't have wanted it any other way. I wouldn't be the only one infuriated. His bowling colleagues must surely have been, Farokh dropping a simple catch one minute and taking a breath-taking one-hander the next!

He has hit centuries all around the world – Calcutta, Bombay, Perth, Brisbane and Swansea! Yet he had to wait until 1975, before he notched his one and only 'ton' at Old Trafford against Warwickshire. Farokh has sacrificed his wicket many a time for his side and there aren't too many cricketers who will do that. The 'Roses' match as Sheffield's Bramall Lane in 1969 was the scene of a performance which perhaps typifies the man. Farokh had scored 96 when he tried to reach his hundred by hitting a six. He lashed out to a ball bowled by Geoff Cope and gave a simple catch to mid-on. He walked back to the pavilion muttering something like "Rookie, you silly man! What makes you do these daft things?"

On his retirement, he became a marketing executive with a textile firm, making his home in Lancashire where he has made so many friends.

William Farrimond

Birthplace:	Daisy Hill, Bolton
Born:	23rd May 1903
Died:	14th November 1979
Played:	1924–1945

Averages in all first-class Lancashire matches

Matches	Innings	Not Outs	Runs	Highest Score	Average	100s	50s
134	142	38	2,202	63	21.17	—	13

Runs	Wickets	Caught	Stumped	Total
16	0	232	65	297

Number of Test Appearances – 4

BILL FARRIMOND joined Lancashire in 1924, just at the time George Duckworth was at his peak. He therefore spent many years as Duckworth's understudy. Duckworth did not give up his regular position until the late 1930s, so Farrimond's opportunities were limited. Yet, as he approached the end of his career, Duckworth was always willing to step down and let Farrimond gain more experience.

If he had been playing the game today, Farrimond would probably have moved to another first-class county to ensure a first-team place. It speaks volumes for Farrimond's loyalty that during this long period as Duckworth's understudy he never accepted any of the offers he received to qualify for another county.

Against Kent in 1930 at Old Trafford, he equalled what was then the world record by claiming seven victims in an innings, catching six and stumping one. He toured South Africa with the M.C.C. in 1930-31 and kept wicket in the last two Tests at Johannesburg and Durban. It was a measure of the high regard in which his wicket-keeping was held that Farrimond also played in the Second Test against the West Indies at Port of Spain in 1935 and in the Second Test against South Africa at Lords, each time when Les Ames was also in the team.

He never made a century in the county first team but in 1934 he hit 174 for the Minor Counties against Oxford University. In 1938, when

Duckworth called it a day, Farrimond stepped into his shoes. Then came the Second World War and, by the end of it, he was too old for the first-class game. In all, he claimed 297 victims, in a quiet, efficient manner. He then returned to his native Westhoughton to play in the side which won the Bolton League Championshipsin 1940, 1941, 1942 and 1943.

If batting had been considered an important criterion of selection, as it often is today, Farrimond, a sound and confident wicket-keeper, may have ousted Duckworth, for Farrimond was the better batsman.

Graeme Fowler

Birthplace:	Accrington
Born:	20th April 1957
Died:	—
Played:	1979–

Averages in all first-class Lancashire matches

Matches	Innings	Not Outs	Runs	Highest Score	Average	100s	50s
159	267	17	9,450	226	37.80	21	46

Runs	Wickets	Average	Best	5 Wickets	10 Wickets
117	5	23.40	2-34	—	—

Number of Test Appearances – 21

GRAEME FOWLER did not start to play cricket until he was twelve years of age. Whilst on holiday in Devon, his father got him to bat and, once back home, coaching lessons in the garden followed. Within three years, Fowler was the youngest batsman in the Lancashire League, where he first appeared for his home town team, Accrington, and then Rawtenstall.

He first played for the County Second XI at the age of 16, in 1973. During 1975 and 1976,

Graeme represented the England Schools Cricket Association, M.C.C. Schools and Young England – all this as a wicket-keeper batsman. In 1976, he was the Lancashire Cricket Federation Young Cricketer of the Year. Like Paul Allott, he atended Durham University and, in 1978, he left as a qualified P.E. teacher and joined Lancashire on a full-time basis. His hopes were soon dashed, however, as he injured his foot in a car crash and was out of the game for several months.

He spent that winter in Australia, working as a groundsman and playing for the Scarborough Club in Perth. He admitted that, initially, the pace and bounce were too much for him, but he returned to Lancashire and, through being less committed to the front foot, averaged 40 as an opening batsman. Two years after making his county debut in 1979, he was awarded his county cap, scoring 1,560 runs throughout the season. The following year, 1982, Fowler scored consistently well for Lancashire and earned himself an England cap, against Pakistan. In the second innings of that match, he top scored with 86, holding Imran Khan at bay.

As has been mentioned, Graeme was a very useful wicket-keeper in his early days and occupied that position in many Lancashire one-day matches, but it is really in the field – in any position – that he excels.

Graeme is a left-handed opening batsman who hits the ball extremely hard. He was represented his country on twenty-one occasions, a total I feel that he has been unlucky not to add to.

Tommy Greenhough

Birthplace:	Rochdale
Born:	9th November 1931
Died:	—
Played:	1951–1966

Averages in all first-class Lancashire matches

Matches	Innings	Not Outs	Runs	Highest Score	Average	100s	50s
241	298	79	1,868	76*	8.52	—	1

Runs	Wickets	Average	Best	5 Wickets	10 Wickets
15,540	707	21.98	7-56	32	5

Number of Test Appearances – 4

TOMMY GREENHOUGH started his first-class career in 1951. In many respects, he was born a generation too late – he was a cricketing artist. He was a cheery, bouncing sort of chap, happy to be alive; yet, when he donned a pair of flannels, he became the arch-deceiver.

Greenhough was a right-handed leg-break bowler who used to run in a long way for such a bowler, with bouncing strides and the ball held in both hands until delivery. Greenhough could spin the ball considerably and took no fewer than 707 wickets in his time with Lancashire. He took 100 wickets in a season twice and went on two tours. In 1956-57, he toured Jamaica with the Duke of Norfolk's team and in 1959-60 he went with the M.C.C. to the West Indies.

Throughout the 1950s and 1960s, when Greenhough (who was an outstanding exponent of his art) was bowling well for Lancashire, it didn't always bring his the corrent rewards. Leg-break bowling in England, unfortunately for Greenhough, was becoming a dying art. Both selectors and umpires began to mistrust him. He did represent England on four occasions, however, and, on one of his appearances, against India at Lords, he took five for thirty-five.

Greenhough suffered the misfortune of having his career curtailed in 1966, due to injuries to both hands and feet. In fact, his career was one long battle against cricketing odds – on and off the field. He was hospitalised for two lengthy spells in his career; one, when he was playing as deputy professional in the Lancashire League when he almost lost a finger trying to field a shot from Frank Worrell; the other occasion was when he fell down a lift-shaft and broke both ankles!

Ken Grieves

Birthplace:	Sydney, Australia
Born:	27th August 1925
Died:	—
Played:	1949–1964

Averages in all first-class Lancashire matches

Matches	Innings	Not Outs	Runs	Highest Score	Average	100s	50s
452	696	73	20,802	224	33.39	26	129

Runs	Wickets	Average	Best	5 Wickets	10 Wickets
6,769	235	28.80	6–60	8	—

Number of Test Appearances – 0

IN HIS NATIVE Australia, Ken Grieves first played for the Ashfield Junior Technical School and while there was selected to represent the New South Wales schoolboys, following which he played for one of the Sydney Central schools for a couple of seasons. He eventually went on to represent the full New South Wales state side.

He played for Lancashire from 1949 to 1961. He fit 1,000 runs in a season no less than 13 times, plus one in India in 1950-51 when he represented the

Commonwealth on a tour to the east.

His three double-centuries were all made whilst playing for Lancashire. His worth to his county was immeasurable, being one of only a handful of players to surpass 20,000 runs in his career.

In 1962, he left the county scene and returned to League cricket as professional with Stockport. He was persuaded to return as captain for the following two seasons.

Ken Grieves bowled leg-breaks and 'googlies' – accuracy was not his strength but he was resourceful and had the happy knack of getting good wickets quickly and cheaply.

Grieves was also a Football League goalkeeper, playing for both Bury and Bolton Wanderers.

His cricket can be summed up by saying that he had a natural instinct for the game – he knew automatically what to do and when to do it.

Charlie Hallows

Birthplace:	Little Lever, Bolton
Born:	4th April 1895
Died:	10th November 1972
Played:	1914–1932

Averages in all first-class Lancashire matches

Matches	Innings	Not Outs	Runs	Highest Score	Average	100s	50s
370	569	62	20,142	233*	39.72	52	92

Runs	Wickets	Average	Best	5 Wickets	10 Wickets
84	19	41.26	3–28	—	—

Number of Test Appearances – 2

CHARLIE HALLOWS first played for Lancashire in 1914 as a left-arm bowler but it was as a batsman that he made his mark in Lancashire cricket.

From 1919–1930, he passed the 1,000 run mark each season and in 1925, 1927 and 1928, he topped 2,000 runs. In 1928, the best year of his Lancashire career, he scored over 2,500 runs at an average of 65. It was in 1928 that he achieved a place in cricket records when he became only the third player (along with W. G. Grace and Wally Hammond) to score a thousand runs in the month of May.

In fact, when the match against Sussex began at Old Trafford on 30th May, Hallows still needed to score 232 runs to complete his thousand. He batted all through the first day and was 190 not out at the close of play. He reached his target the following morning, but the very next ball he received after reaching his thousand runs, he was out, caught. In all, Hallows hit eleven centuries for Lancashire that summer.

In 1929, he had the distinction of carrying his bat through the Lancashire innings in the Old Trafford 'Roses' match. Lancashire started badly and at one stage were 14 for 3, but Hallows with some help from George Duckworth helped avoid a complete collapse. Hallows finished on 152 not out.

Hallows was a fine county batsman and will always be remembered for the important contributions he made to Lancashire winning the County Championship in 1926, 1927 and 1928.

As an opening batsman, he took his responsibilities very seriously indeed. He was very cautious initially but, after he had helped lay a solid foundation for the rest of the innings, he was able to revert to a more adventurous role, always giving the impression that he enjoyed his batting.

His favourite stroke was the straight drive and he was also especially strong on the on-side, always putting plenty of power into his shots.

He was perhaps a little unfortunate to play only twice for his country, against Australia in 1921 and then, seven years later, against the West Indies.

Below: Sutcliffe and Hallows open for England against the West Indies at Lord's in 1928.

Hallows also had the distinction of holding posts as a cricket professional in England, Ireland, Scotland and Wales!

In his later years, after he'd been Chief Coach to Worcestershire County Cricket Club, when they'd won the County Championship, he returned to Manchester as Chief Coach. The players he had in his charge at that time went on to play under Jack Bond and gain success in the one-day game.

Frank Hayes

Birthplace:	Preston
Born:	6th December 1946
Died:	—
Played:	1970–1984

Averages in all first-class Lancashire matches

Matches	Innings	Not Outs	Runs	Highest Score	Average	100s	50s
22	339	48	10,899	187	37.45	22	52

Runs	Wickets	Average	Best	5 Wickets	10 Wickets
11	0	—	—	—	—

Number of Test Appearances – 9

FRANK HAYES Senior was a cricket-mad father, wanting the best for his son. He began by laying a concrete strip in the back garden, covering it with matting and erecting a net. Every spare moment, Frank practised with his father.

Even before he'd reached the age of 10, Frank was playing for Marple in the High Peak Junior League, against boys not far short of 17. Father and son opened the innings and despite Frank running out his father, the progress didn't end there.

At the age of 14, he was representing the Marple first eleven in the Lancashire and Cheshire League. Three years later, he represented Cheshire in a match against Lancashire. He made 37 before Jack Bond claimed the catch off Ken Higgs bowling.

Sadly, Frank Senior had now died, but Frank kept his promise that he would secure his future before contemplating a first-class cricket career. He went to Sheffield University, obtaining a degree in Mathematics and Physics and representing them at rugby and soccer as well as cricket. He had played for the county second eleven for four years and when he was eventually persuaded to sign for Lancashire, it was not without any doubts. "I couldn't see how I could possibly get in the first team and the best I hoped for was to get my second eleven cap within two years."

Frank made his first team debut against Middlesex at Old Trafford, replacing Clive Lloyd who was representing the Rest of the World side against England. Frank had taken two slip catches on the first day, but it was on day two that Frank walked out to bat, with Lancashire standing on 47–4. It soon became 57–5 and then Frank was joined by Ken Snellgrove. Frank weathered the blistering pace of John Price and the spin of Fred Titmus. The debut 'ton' wasn't to be. He fell six short on 94, but there was still a rapturous welcome from the members' enclosure.

Frank was regarded as the 'great white hope' of English cricket. Unfortunately, despite a successful career by most standards, he was one of the major disappointments of modern first-class cricket.

Everyone who has seen Frank bat seemed convinced that he had the ability of a potentially great player. Everyone, possibly, that is, except Frank himself.

He once said, "I'm sure I have played against most of the county bowlers and scored runs off them – I think the weakness is in my own mind. I tend to think about my batting a lot." He went on, "If I'm going through a bad patch, I feel it's almost as if I have forgotten what it feels like to play well, to play naturally."

In 1973, he was selected to represent his country in the test series against the West Indies and in the second innings of his debut, scored 106 not out. Hayes went on to play for England on nine occasions, unfortunately all of them against the great West Indies. In fact, in the series in the Caribbean, Hayes was physically sick before going in to bat and never regained his English place.

His highest score for Lancashire was 187 at Old Trafford against India and in the County Championship 157 against Nottinghamshire at Trent Bridge.

Hayes proved on many occasions that he really did possess a rare talent. He once hit the Glamorgan bowler Malcolm Nask for 34 runs in one over!

Ken Higgs

Birthplace:	Kidsgrove
Born:	14th January 1937
Died:	—
Played:	1958–1969

Averages in all first-class Lancashire matches

Matches	Innings	Not Outs	Runs	Highest Score	Average	100s	50s
306	374	131	2,655	60	10.92	—	1

Runs	Wickets	Average	Best	5 Wickets	10 Wickets
23,661	1,033	22.90	7–19	37	5

Number of Test Appearances – 15

KEN HIGGS came to the county game on an abundance of natural ability. He played both cricket and soccer for the Secondary School in Tunstall and lived only a few yards from the Meakins Pottery Works. One evening he was asked to make up the numbers for the Potteries 2nd XI. This he did, and though he was not quite 12 years old, he ended the game as their top scorer! At 15, he joined Port Vale, playing centre half for the reserves and actually having one game for the first team.

He soon joined Lancashire and made a startling debut in 1958 against Hampshire, taking 7–36 off 9 overs. He often opened with Brian Statham and together they were probably the best opening pair on the county scene. Higgs learned much from Statham – control of line and flight most certainly.

Ken Higgs won 15 England caps, taking 71 wickets at a little over 20 runs each. He was no mug with the bat either, he once scored 63 in a last wicket partnership with John Snow against the West Indies in 1966. His batting could probably be described as stubborn, yet he did score 98 after leaving Lancashire. He put on 228 for the last wicket with Ray Illingworth during his time with Leicestershire.

Ken Higgs was a well built right-arm medium-fast bowler. He had a short approach to the wicket but had a strong thrusting body-action, resulting in quite a quick delivery off the pitch. Higgs took two first-class 'hat-tricks' in his years at Old Trafford and two more with Leicesterhire, including one in the 1974 Benson and Hedges Cup Final.

Higgs' accuracy and pace resulted in him being one of the most respected and successful bowlers in county cricket. He is now using his wealth of experience to the full at Grace Road, where he is the county coach.

Malcolm Hilton

Birthplace:	Chadderton
Born:	2nd August 1928
Died:	—
Played:	1946–1961

Averages in all first-class Lancashire matches

Matches	Innings	Not Outs	Runs	Highest Score	Average	100s	50s
241	294	35	3,140	100*	12.12	1	5

Runs	Wickets	Average	Best	5 Wickets	10 Wickets
17,419	926	18.81	8-19	48	8

Number of Test Appearances – 4

MALCOLM HILTON joined the county club in 1946 and shot to fame in 1948, when in the tour match against Australia at Old Trafford, he dismissed the great Don Bradman twice!

However, the following year, he was back in the County Second XI! But he did take more wickets than any other bowler – he took over 100 which was a very unusual feat in Minor County cricket. On a turning wicket, Malcolm Hilton was as devastating a left-arm spinner as you're likely to see.

His best season was in 1956; he took 158 wickets at just under 14 runs each. Hilton was also a superb fielder, both close-in and in the outfield, where his great speed and accuracy in throwing resulted in many run-outs. With all these credentials, he was often chosen as England's twelfth man. However, he did actually represent England on four occasions.

His best bowling for Lancashire was 8–19 against the touring New Zealanders in 1958. Hilton was a very handy batsman; he was an aggressive tail-ender with a slashing off-drive that resulted in just one century, 100 not out, against Northamptonshire.

Len Hopwood

Birthplace:	Newton Hyde
Born:	30th October 1903
Died:	15th June 1985
Played:	1923–1939

Averages in all first-class Lancashire matches

Matches	Innings	Not Outs	Runs	Highest Score	Average	100s	50s
397	571	54	15,519	220	30.01	27	70

Runs	Wickets	Average	Best	5 Wickets	10 Wickets
14,905	672	22.18	9–33	35	6

Number of Test Appearances – 2

LEN HOPWOOD was taken to the Old Trafford nets in the early 1920's where one of his mentors was the great Archie MacLaren. The famous Red-Rose batsman took one look at the frail Hopwood and observed "To be an all-rounder you have to be as strong as an ox and a bloody fool, and you are neither."

Hopwood made his county debut in 1923 and went on to prove MacLaren wrong. However, he arrived on the scene as Lancashire were winning the County Championship three years on the trot and so he took a few years to establish himself in the county team. In fact he played for Cheshire in the 1926 and 1927 seasons.

Hopwood was a lively all-rounder. He replaced Cecil Parkin in the 1928 team and the post his own and held it in the 1930 side as well. Hopwood was a good right-handed batsman and a left-arm medium-pace bowler.

In 1933, he scored 1,972 runs at an average of 46.96 and in 1934 he took 111 wickets at a cost of 20.69 including 9–69. Hopwood was the only cricketer to achieve the double of 1,000 runs and 100 wickets more than once for Lancashire and this he did in 1934 and 1935. He scored runs when they were badly needed and took wickets on a regular basis.

Hopwood went on to play for England on two occasions both against Australia, at Old Trafford and Headingley. He was very disappointing, scoring only 12 runs and not taking a wicket. If he could have produced his county form he may well have made many more appearances.

When war broke out in 1939, Hopwood had scored 15,519 runs and taken 672 wickets. When cricket resumed after the war, ill-health thwarted his return to the first-class game. He then became assistant-coach, administrator and consultant at Old Trafford. In 1981, he became President of the County Club. At the time of his death in 1985, he was the oldest surviving capped player for Lancashire.

Albert Hornby

Birthplace:	Blackburn
Born:	10th February 1847
Died:	17th December 1925
Played:	1867–1899

Averages in all first-class Lancashire matches

Matches	Innings	Not Outs	Runs	Highest Score	Average	100s	50s
292	467	28	10,649	188	24.25	10	49

Runs	Wickets	Average	Best	5 Wickets	10 Wickets
94	3	31.33	1-2	–	–

Number of Test Appearances – 3

ALBERT NEILSON HORNBY, nicknamed 'Monkey', was born in Blackburn in 1847. He first came to the fore when playing for Harrow against Eton in 1864 at the age of 17, at Lord's. He was described as 'the little wonder', the smallest player ever seen on the ground, weighing under six stone – and that included the bat!

He first played for Lancashire in 1867 and within two years, had become a first-team regular. He was well-equipped for leadership and became county captain in 1880. He captained the county side for twelve seasons from 1880–1891. He shared the captaincy with S.M. Crosfield in 1892 and 1893 and was then persuaded to accept the office again in 1897.

Albert Hornby feared no-one and had no time for anyone who wasn't prepared to give of his best. He had a complete understanding of each of his players and won and retained their admiration and respect.

As a captain, he drove his team hard and was a stickler for discipline. He would set a fine example in the field and woe betide any player who didn't pull his weight.

When the young Archie MacLaren arrived fresh from Harrow to play for Lancashire, he had the gall to suggest he would field anywhere, but not at point. Hornby had no hesitation, the young MacLaren was sent directly to point!

During Hornby's captaincy, the Red Rose fielding became legendary. As with everything Hornby was connected with, there was more than a touch of aggression about Lancashire's fielding. Hornby was a strong forward player, often playing with aggression from the very first ball bowled. His opening partner, Barlow, was the opposite, a model of patience – they complimented each other very well indeed.

'Monkey' Hornby hit sixteen centuries for Lancashire, his highest score being 188 against Derbyshire at Old Trafford in 1881. He represented his country at home and in Australia. His test record isn't special, though he did display two instances of courage.

In 1878, he played in the game that Australia won inside a day. In the England second innings, Spofforth hit Hornby. Spofforth bowled like lightning and the majority of batsmen hit by him did not return for a second go! Hornby, realising his side was in deep trouble, showed great bravery by resuming his innings – an act that was very much appreciated by the large crowd.

In 1879 in Australia, the crowd at the Melbourne Cricket Ground invaded the field of play, incensed by an umpiring decision. Lord Harris, the England captain, was hit by a spectator. Hornby too was hit and his shirt was torn from his back, but it didn't stop him from seizing the ringleader and marching him off to the pavilion and into the arms of the law.

Hornby was a double internationalist. He represented his country three times at cricket and nine times at Rugby Football. He also captained England twice at cricket, at the Oval in the 1882 legendary test and two years later at Old Trafford. He was also given the honour of leading out his country in his last Rugby International appearance against Scotland. For good measure, he also played soccer for Blackburn Rovers!

When Hornby finally called it a day, his talent was by no means lost to Red Rose cricket. He was President of the County Club from 1894 to 1916. Even when he died in 1925, he still had the interests of Lancashire cricket at heart.

Nigel Howard

Birthplace:	Preston
Born:	18th May 1925
Died:	31st May 1979
Played:	1946–1953

Averages in all first-class Lancashire matches

Matches	Innings	Not Outs	Runs	Highest Score	Average	100s	50s
170	234	29	5,526	145	26.95	3	33

Runs	Wickets	Average	Best	5 Wickets	10 Wickets
23	0	—	—	—	—

Number of Test Appearances – 4

NIGEL HOWARD was one of two sons of Major Rupert Howard, a former Lancashire secretary and manager of M.C.C. touring teams.

Nigel was at Rossall School during the early part of the war and was a highly rated player, capable of scoring his half-century frequently. His highest score at this level was 135 not out against Alleyns in 1942.

He first appeared for the county in 1946, but it was two years later, before he obtained a regular place. It was this year, 1948, that he hit the highest score of his career, 145 at Old Trafford against Derbyshire.

In 1949, at the age of 24, Nigel Howard became not only the youngest Red-Rose captain, but also the most criticised. This criticism was not fair, though, for Howard skippered Lancashire for five seasons, and they were in the main successful ones.

In 1950, greatly helped by Cyril Washbrook, he led Lancashire to the joint County Championship and to third position for the next three years. At the same time, Howard was instrumental in rebuilding the team, putting his faith in the youngsters – Bob Berry, Brian Statham and Roy Tattersall. His best seasons were 1948, when he scored 944 runs at an average of 36.30, and 1950 when his aggregate was 1,124 runs and his average 36.68.

Howard represented his country on four occasions, captaining the M.C.C. team to India and Pakistan, in 1951–52. For Lancashire, Howard was a very stylish batsman and could hit the ball extremely hard, but he struggled to keep his place in the England team.

Howard though, does have a rare claim to fame. Twice during his days as Lancashire captain, did the county win Championship matches within a day. He missed the first at Bath against Somerset, but he was in charge when Lancashire thrashed Sussex by an innings in 1950.

He retired from first-class cricket in 1953 in order to devote himself to the family textile business.

David Hughes

Birthplace:		Newton-le-Willows
Born:		13th May 1947
Died:		—
Played:		1967–

Averages in all first-class Lancashire matches

Matches	Innings	Not Outs	Runs	Highest Score	Average	100s	50s
389	513	91	9,293	153	22.02	8	41

Runs	Wickets	Average	Best	5 Wickets	10 Wickets
17,505	596	29.37	7–24	20	2

Number of Test Appearances – 0

DAVID HUGHES made his debut at Old Trafford against Oxford University in 1967. Running up to bowl his first ball, his feet went from under him and he was left sprawling at the umpires feet.

Before joining Lancashire, he had spent two seasons playing for his home town team Newton-le-Willows in the Manchester Association and three years with Farnworth in the Bolton League.

His first ever County Championship wicket was that of Colin Cowdrey at Canterbury in the fixture against Kent. David still holds Lancashire's bowling record in the Sunday League, taking 6–29 against Somerset in 1977.

He is a right-handed lower order batsman with an ability to play hard-hitting innings. He is also (although not so much nowadays) a slow left-arm bowler who has been most useful to the County throughout his career and as a fielder, has taken some breath-taking catches.

David of course is remembered throughout the world for one vital over that turned the tide for Lancashire in the Gillette Cup Semi-Final of 1971 against Gloucestershire. The bowler was John Mortimore and David Hughes was the hero, hammering 24 runs – 4-6-2-2-4-6!

David also took 26 off an over bowled by Bishen Bedi in the 1976 Gillette Cup Final against Northamptonshire, unfortunately not with the same winning result.

In 1981 and 1982, he scored over 1,000 runs for Lancashire, but the 153 he made against Glamorgan at Old Trafford in 1983 remains his highest score. In 1986, he and Alan Ormrod captained the Second Team and led them to the 2nd XI County Championship.

More recently of course, David has become 1st team skipper and has transformed the County Championship side into one which we hope will be this year's champions, especially after coming so close in 1987.

Jack Iddon

Birthplace:	Mawdesley
Born:	8th January 1902
Died:	17th April 1946
Played:	1924–1945

Averages in all first-class Lancashire matches

Matches	Innings	Not Outs	Runs	Highest Score	Average	100s	50s
483	683	90	21,975	222	37.05	46	105

Runs	Wickets	Average	Best	5 Wickets	10 Wickets
14,214	533	26.66	9–42	14	2

Number of Test Appearances – 5

JACK IDDON was born at Mawdesley, near Ormskirk, in 1902, the son of a professional cricketer. Cricket was part and parcel of the family atmosphere. When Jack was in his teens, he played many good innings and took wickets in plenty for both Neston and Leyland Motors Cricket Clubs.

In 1922, he became a professional cricketer for Lancashire. His period of apprenticeship to the game wasn't of long duration. He made his debut two years later. There wasn't, however, anything sensational in his arrival to the first-class game.

It was thought during his early days with Lancashire that he would become the long-awaited successor to Johnny Briggs, but whilst he did end his career with 533 wickets, it was obvious for all to see that he was too good a batsman to devote too much time to his bowling.

In 1926, he topped the 1,000 run mark for the first time and his batting was beginning to flourish. As a batsman, Iddon had plenty of strokes. His off-drives were graceful, his leg-glances neat, his pulls fiercesome and his cutting magnificent, but the one synonymous with his name is the straight drive.

The encounters with Yorkshire seemed to bring the best out in him. He hit 142 not out at Old Trafford in 1934 and took 9–42 at Sheffield in 1937. He hit a thousand runs or more in twelve consecutive seasons up to the start of the second World War.

He hit 46 centuries, including 4 double centuries. In fact, he hit centuries against all other first-class cricketing counties – a very impressive record indeed.

Iddon represented his country on five occasions, all in the 1935 home series against South Africa. His highest score was 73 and he ended the series with an average of nearly 30 – not brilliant, but certainly not a failure.

During the war, Jack Iddon turned his attention to business. However, he didn't neglect his cricket. He organised games on behalf of war charities and travelled miles to give relief to workers and keep the game of cricket alive despite the difficulties imposed by the war. Iddon sacrificed his leisure time to play cricket, even the Sabbath was not his own – for during the war, this was the only time war workers were free. He saw to it that they had good cricket to watch and the British Red Cross Association benefitted from the proceeds taken at these matches.

The death of Jack Iddon on 18th April 1946 was a terrible blow to Lancashire cricket. A motor accident in the evening saw Iddon killed instantaneously. Lancashire had lost a great cricketer.

Jack Ikin

Birthplace:	Bignall End
Born:	7th March 1918
Died:	15th September 1984
Played:	1939–1957

Averages in all first-class Lancashire matches

Matches	Innings	Not Outs	Runs	Highest Score	Average	100s	50s
288	431	51	14,327	192	37.70	23	86

Runs	Wickets	Average	Best	5 Wickets	10 Wickets
8,005	278	28.79	6–21	10	1

Number of Test Appearances – 18

JACK IKIN made his Lancashire debut in the 1939 season, playing four matches in all. His first wicket in first-class cricket was that of the great George Headley.

Jack Ikin was a genuine all-rounder. He was a left-handed batsman, showing an assertive grace when playing his shots. He often had to shore up many of Lancashire's innings after early wickets had fallen, whether he was opening or batting at number six or seven. His slow right-handed bowling looked very easy from the pavilion, but was anything but! The mixture of leg-breaks and googlies confusing many a good batsman. Ikin was also a brilliant fielder, especially in the short-leg or slip area.

Against Somerset at Taunton in 1949, Ikin did the 'hat-trick' and two years later, in 1951, he scored the highest score of his career, 192 against Oxford University.

He made his England debut before he had received his county cap. He passed 1,000 runs on no fewer than eleven occasions. His best season was 1952, when he scored 1,912 runs at an average of 45.52.

Towards the end, he missed quite a lot of cricket due to ill-health and it was this, that forced him to retire in 1957. However, his career was far from over. He rejoined Staffordshire and continued to play for them until 1968, including ten years as captain.

Ikin was also assistant manager to S. C. Griffiths on the M.C.C. tour of

Australia and New Zealand in 1965-66 and in 1972 he managed the first England Young Cricketers' side to the West Indies.

For many years he was coach at Denstone School, where he was a much loved and respected figure and was elected an Honorary Cricketing Member of the M.C.C.

Peter Lever

Birthplace:	Todmorden
Born:	17th September 1940
Died:	—
Played:	1960–1976

Averages in all first-class Lancashire matches

Matches	Innings	Not Outs	Runs	Highest Score	Average	100s	50s
268	285	59	3,073	83	13.59	—	9

Runs	Wickets	Average	Best	5 Wickets	10 Wickets
17,647	716	24.64	7-70	25	2

Number of Test Appearances – 17

PETER LEVER was a Lancashire League player with Todmorden, his home town team, and, performing well, he was invited to Old Trafford for a trial as a batsman! He was later invited to play for the second eleven as a bowler!

During his time with Todmorden, Peter spent five years in the first team and two years with the second team, this time as a wicket-keeper!

He made his Lancashire debut against Cambridge University. Lancashire batted all the first day, it rained the second and he took 0–22 on the third – not the best of debut games.

Peter Lever was an aggressive right-arm bowler and, at times, a more than useful batsman. He bowled with a fierce pace and was more successful when he pitched the ball up and used the seam. Lever's secret weapon was a very late out-swinger which defeated many great batsmen.

Occasionally, he would dig the ball in to produce the bouncer, but this ploy was reduced somewhat when, in 1975, a delivery of his almost killed the New Zealander number eleven, Ewen Chatfield.

'Plank', as he was affectionately known, was a late developer. He was thirty years old when he toured Australia as an important part of the 1971 side to bring back the Ashes. Prior to this, he had represented England against the Rest of the World and took 7–83. I remember seeing him score 88 not out against India at Old Trafford, sharing a record stand with Ray

Illingworth, just another reminder that he was certainly no mug with the bat.

Four years later in Melbourne, he took 6–38 and was the ideal partner for John Snow. Unfortunately, Lever suffered greatly with back trouble and it was this that forced his retirement sooner than he would have preferred.

Clive Lloyd

Birthplace:	Georgetown, Guyana	
Born:	3st August 1944	
Died:	–	
Played:	1968–1986	

Averages in all first-class Lancashire matches

Matches	Innings	Not Outs	Runs	Highest Score	Average	100s	50s
219	326	42	12,764	217*	44.94	30	71

Runs	Wickets	Average	Best	5 Wickets	10 Wickets
1,809	55	32.89	4–48	—	—

Number of Test Appearances – 110 (West Indies)

CLIVE HUBERT LLOYD was born in Georgetown, Guyana. At school when 12 years old, he was trying to separate two school chums who were fighting. He received an accidental blow in the eye and his eyesight was affected. He has worn spectacles ever since. His father also died whilst Clive was still at school and he combined being the bread-winner of the family with establishing himself as a cricketer.

He came to England in 1967 and played as professional for Haslingden in the Lancashire League. When his Haslingden contract expired, he accepted an offer to play for Lancashire.

His early years with Lancashire were very successful in terms of one-day cricket. Clive still holds the club record for the highest individual scores in the Sunday League: 134 not out against Somerset in 1970 and in the Benson and Hedges Cup; 124 against Warwickshire in 1981. Those of us who saw his masterly innings of 126 against Warwickshire in the Gillette Cup Final, will remember it for ever.

When Gillette ended their sponsorship in 1980, Clive Lloyd was awarded the 'Man of the Series' trophy. He was appointed captain of the West Indies in 1974–75 and he celebrated this with his highest test score of 242 not out against India at Bombay. He was appointed captain of Lancashire in 1981 – captaincy never affected his batting, he was always very consistent.

Clive hit 6 centuries against Yorkshire in 'Roses' matches, at present a record. His highest County Championship score was 217 not out against Warwickshire at Old Trafford in 1971 – surely his favourite county!

Clive represented the West Indies on 110 occasions, scoring 7,515 runs at an average of 46.67 and 19 centuries. Clive was a calm and able skipper, who not only led his country to World Cup success on two occasions, but also to numerous Test series victories. In fact, Clive still holds the record for the most Test innings before scoring a 'duck' – 58!

Before he had operations on both knees, he patrolled the covers like a panther. He had speed, safe hands, a long reach and an accurate return – for me, the greatest cover-point of all time and there have been some great ones at Old Trafford.

Even his medium-paced bowling, which he developed in League cricket, brought him wickets at both county and test levels, often breaking the most stubborn of partnerships.

Clive certainly enjoyed his cricket and we spectators certainly enjoyed watching him play it. The prospect of seeing Clive play brought the crowds flocking to the grounds, whether it be Old Trafford or Buxton. Clive would time the ball and generate immense power in his strokes. A big man, Clive had the heaviest bat in cricket (over 3 lbs in weight!).

It cannot and should not be too long before Clive becomes Sir Clive for his services to both Lancashire and the West Indies.

David Lloyd

Birthplace:	Accrington
Born:	18th March 1947
Died:	—
Played:	1965–1983

Averages in all first-class Lancashire matches

Matches	Innings	Not Outs	Runs	Highest Score	Average	100s	50s
378	605	70	17,877	195	33.41	37	86

Runs	Wickets	Average	Best	5 Wickets	10 Wickets
7,007	234	29.94	7–38	5	1

Number of Test Appearances – 9

DAVID LLOYD made his Lancashire debut in 1965. He went on to become a superb all-round cricketer. He was compact, strong and left-handed, more often than not opening the innings. He was a batsman who had all the shots, often playing with exceptional flair. Coupled with his slow left-arm spin, often under used, and a brilliant close field, he was a great asset to the county club.

David Lloyd or 'Bumble' (due to the fact that he talks incessantly and with an engaging Lancashire burr) was the county captain between 1973 and 1977. It was under David Lloyd's cheerful leadership that Lancashire reached three successive Gillette Cup Finals, winning in 1975. His all-round ability is shown in his final figures for Lancashire – 17,877 runs and 234 wickets. Graeme Fowler, Lancashire's present opening batsman has much to thank David Lloyd for.

Lloyd played for England on nine occasions and despite having to face the pace and tenacity of Dennis Lillee and Jeff Thomson in their prime, he ended his test career with an average of 42.46. Lloyd played spin beautifully, and never more so than when he scored 214 not out at Edgbaston against India. Bishen Bedi and the other Indian bowlers had no answer to Lloyd's cutting, driving and pulling, which were all based on his neat footwork.

At the time of writing, Lloyd is on the Umpires Panel and his son, Graham, a very promising opening bat, is waiting to follow in dad's footsteps!

Archie MacLaren

Birthplace:	Whalley Range
Born:	1st December 1871
Died:	17th November 1944
Played:	1890–1914

Averages in all first-class Lancashire matches

Matches	Innings	Not Outs	Runs	Highest Score	Average	100s	50s
307	510	37	15,772	424	33.34	30	72

Runs	Wickets	Average	Best	5 Wickets	10 Wickets
247	1	247.00	1–44	—	—

Number of Test Appearances – 35

ARCHIE MACLAREN was a Manchester man by birth, though his family came from Scotland. His father James was, in fact, Treasurer and later President of the County Club. In his early years, Archie spent much of his time at Old Trafford benefiting from some careful coaching and putting in some hard work to become a great batsman.

Before going to Harrow, he was coached at Elstree by Vernon Royle, possibly the greatest cover-point Lancashire have had. So when he did arrive at Harrow, he had both natural talent and wisdom. Whilst at Harrow and at the age of fifteen, he scored 55 and 67 in the match against Eton.

He made his Lancashire debut in 1890 at Brighton, taking 108 off the Sussex attack after the Red-Rose county had been 23–3. The following year, he only played five games, but still topped the county batting averages.

S. M. Crosfield was appointed captain for the 1894 season, but was unable to undertake the role. So the Committee appointed Archie MacLaren to take over, though he was only 22 years old. Of the first seven fixtures, Lancashire won only one, losing the other six – not the brightest of starts! In 1895 though, there was a marked improvement, with Lancashire finishing as runners-up to Surrey in the County Championship. It was in this season, after missing the first two games due to his late arrival in the country from Australia and a further seven games after accepting a job as a schoolmaster, that he put his name in the record books forever! He rejoined the Lancashire team at Taunton for the match against Somerset and, going in first, proceeded to hit the Somerset attack for 424 runs in 7 hours 50 minutes. His innings is still the highest played in first-class cricket in England.

MacLaren led the Lancashire side through the successful period of 1900–1907 and, in 1904, they were unbeaten as County Champions, yet as England captain he failed to win a series (he got his priorities right!).

Whilst MacLaren scored 15,772 runs for Lancashire it must be remembered that in comparing his run aggregate to other Lancashire greats, his were scored on wickets of variable quality – often quite shocking! His strokes were made with an air of authority. Sir Neville Cardus wrote that he "dismissed the ball from his presence" – he was in charge as soon as he reached the crease. Whether he scored a 'duck' or a hundred, no-one could have made it more regally than Archie MacLaren.

He had a high backlift and was a superb straight-driver, cutter and hooker, but his strength lay in his attacking shots played off the back-foot. He scored a high percentage of his runs by forcing good length balls away on the onside.

He was most definitely a player for the big occasions. He played 35 times for England (22 as Captain) scoring almost 2,000 runs at an average of 33. MacLaren hit many hundreds against Australia, performing much better 'Down Under' than at home.

MacLaren was a great student of the game – a very shrewd tactician. As a county captain, he had few equals. He knew the strengths and weaknesses of all county batsmen and the capabilities of all county bowlers. His leadership would most certainly be classed as authoritarian.

Perhaps his greatest triumph came in 1921 at the ripe old age of 49. The Australians, under the leadership of Warwick Armstrong, were winning everything in sight. MacLaren, who had retired from active cricket, vowed that he could pick a side to beat the victorious Australians. He called it 'An England XI' – it being composed entirely of amateurs. Despite being shot out for 43 in their first innings, the England XI won by 28 runs!

Archie MacLaren was a tremendous force in Lancashire cricket – a genius!

Below: Harry Makepeace

Harry Makepeace

Birthplace:	Middlesborough
Born:	22nd August 1881
Died:	19th December 1952
Played:	1906–1930

Averages in all first-class Lancashire matches

Matches	Innings	Not Outs	Runs	Highest Score	Average	100s	50s
487	757	64	25,207	203	36.37	42	136

Runs	Wickets	Average	Best	5 Wickets	10 Wickets
1,971	42	46.92	4–33	—	—

Number of Test Appearances – 4

HARRY MAKEPEACE played his first game for Lancashire in 1906 and his last in 1930. Towards the end of his career he was appointed assistant-coach and on his retirement, he became Chief Coach to Lancashire.

He was a right-handed opening batsman who relied on timing and placement, very rarely putting much power into his strokes. To him, defence was certainly the best method of attack. It was very difficult to remove him because everything he did at the wicket was done because he felt he was there to stay.

He may have been a defensive-minded player, yet his forward stroke was superbly straight and his footwork quick and sure. He was often in position before the ball reached him and could send the ball wherever he wanted it to go. He was not a stone-waller and certainly not uninteresting to watch.

Makepeace scored over 25,000 runs for Lancashire including 42 centuries. In 1923, he made over 2,000 runs. His highest score, 203 at Worcester, was also made in this season and he followed it up with another double century, 200 not out against Northamptonshire at Aigburth.

In 1926, when the Red-Rose county won the County Championship, Makepeace scored 2,340 runs at an average of 48.75. He hit 1,000 runs or more in thirteen seasons.

He represented England on four occasions, all in the disastrous 1920–21 series in Australia, yet he was one of the few players to come home with any credibility. In the four tests, he scored 279 runs at an average of 34.87, including 117 at Melbourne.

He was another Lancashire cricketer who was a double international, playing soccer for Everton and representing England on one occasion. When Makepeace became coach, it was said that his coaching gave Lancashire a distinctive defensive outlook during the 1930's.

But Harry Makepeace only coached what he had practised during his playing days – that a sound defence is the basis of becoming a good batsman. He spent a lifetime serving Lancashire both on and off the field, always passing on his wisdom to the players who hoped to emulate him.

Ted McDonald

Birthplace:	Launceston (Tasmania)
Born:	6th January 1891
Died:	22nd July 1937
Played:	1924–1931

Averages in all first-class Lancashire matches

Matches	Innings	Not Outs	Runs	Highest Score	Average	100s	50s
217	215	31	1,868	100*	10.15	1	1

Runs	Wickets	Average	Best	5 Wickets	10 Wickets
22,079	1,053	20.96	8–53	94	24

Number of Test Appearances – 11 (Australia)

WHATEVER the period of cricket, Ted McDonald would have been ranked as a great fast bowler. McDonald's action was so perfect that it was always easy to underestimate his speed. His run-up and delivery was smooth and rhythmical and he followed through so fully with his right arm, that there was never any hint of pressing for great pace. Like the majority of great fast bowlers of his day, McDonald didn't normally use the seam in the modern manner, he would rely on spin.

He had represented both Tasmania and Victoria when in 1921 he toured England with Warwick Armstrong's side. In the very first innings of the first game of the tour, it was evident that the Aussies had brought with them a demon bowler. McDonald destroyed Leicestershire by taking 8–41. He finished that series with 27 wickets, at a cost of 24.74 each.

His test career was limited due to his commitment to play for Lancashire. Between 1924 and 1931, he took 1,053 wickets at 20.96 each. This was a remarkable achievement on the easy-paced wickets that prevailed at that time. In fact, at Old Trafford, McDonald was the only bowler who could make the ball rise above stump height. It has been said that McDonald never re-discovered his pace of 1921, but it is not surprising when you consider he was playing six days a week. He may not have been as quick as he was in 1921, but there was certainly more variation to the type of ball he bowled.

McDonald was always the bowler for the great occasion and 'Roses' matches always brought the best out in him.

One player doesn't win a County Championship, even less four in five years, but one surely must admit that McDonald's bowling proved to be a decisive factor. With a game ready to slide into a tame draw, he would snatch victory for Lancashire with an inspired spell of bowling. He was, without doubt, a match-winner and it was this that placed the Red Rose county ahead of their rivals in those winning years.

He first played for Lancashire in 1924, but because of a wet summer and his unavailability, it wasn't until 1925 that the Lancashire supporters saw the best of McDonald. In that season, he took 182 County Championship wickets, 205 in all matches.

In 1926, the first of the Three Championship years, McDonald took 175 wickets. It was also in this season, that McDonald hit his only century in first-class cricket – 100 not out, scored in exactly one hundred minutes!

In 1927, he turned to spin on the wetter pitches and was rewarded with 150 wickets, including 8–73 against Northamptonshire.

His best season was 1928 – he was then 36 years old and, playing in all thirty County Championship games, he took 178 wickets.

In 1929, he took 140 wickets and 108 the following year. It was in 1930, that he claimed the third 'hat-trick' of his career and the great scalp of Don Bradman at Aigburth. In 1931, his contract with Lancashire was mutually terminated and he returned to play in league cricket.

Ted McDonald was tragically killed in 1937 in a motoring accident. He had stopped his own car and was walking back to offer help to the victims of a collision, when he was mown down by another vehicle.

Arthur Mold

Birthplace:	Middleton Cheney, Northants
Born:	27th May 1863
Died:	29th April 1921
Played:	1889–1901

Averages in all first-class Lancashire matches

Matches	Innings	Not Outs	Runs	Highest Score	Average	100s	50s
260	347	114	1,675	57	7.15	—	1

Runs	Wickets	Average	Best	5 Wickets	10 Wickets
23,384	1,543	15.15	9–29	143	53

Number of Test Appearances – 3

ARTHUR MOLD was a Northamptonshire man and he played a few games for his native county before moving to Old Trafford. He first played for Lancashire in 1889 and it wasn't long before he had the reputation of being one of the fastest bowlers in the country. There was, however, a question mark over his action. There seems to be little doubt that on occasions, Mold 'threw', but at that time, the suspicions of 'throwing' hadn't reached the heights it did at the turn of the century. In the following year, Mold, as he had in his first season with the Red Rose took over one hundred wickets, including 9–40 against Yorkshire at Old Trafford.

Arthur Mold was well over six feet in height and had powerful shoulders. He only took seven paces but was genuinely quick, posing problems for all the best batsmen on any type of wicket. In 1892, Mold was chosen as one of Wisden's five cricketers of the year – a great honour. In one particular match that season at Tonbridge against Kent, Mold made the ball fly about so much that he ended up with his career best figures of 9–29.

The following season, 1893, Mold finished with 142 wickets at slightly

over 15 runs each. It was also in this season that Mold made his international debut in three tests against Australia. He didn't, unfortunately, do himself any favours, as he took only seven wickets at over 33 runs each. The following two seasons were Mold's best in terms of first-class cricket matches. In both 1894 and 1895, Mold took over 200 wickets in all matches. In 1894, he took 7–10 against Somerset; this included a hat-trick and then ten balls later, three wickets in four balls. Also in the same season, he took 7–17 against Sussex. In 1895, Mold did Lancashire proud. He took 182 County Championship wickets and lifted the Red Rose county into the runners-up spot. In 1896, Mold bowled while undergoing treatment for a hand injury; he still ended the season with 137 wickets to his name. In the following two seasons, Mold was hampered by injury and, missing several matches, he failed in 1897, for the first time, to reach one hundred wickets. Having said this, he did take 98 wickets and finished eighth in the national averages!

In 1899, Mold's opening partner, Johnny Briggs was injured, so Mold had to bear the brunt of the bowling. He still managed to take 115 wickets. In 1900, he once again narrowly failed to get one hundred wickets, though he did take 97 and finished second to Wilfred Rhodes in the national averages.

Later that year. came the first signs of the trouble that would later end Mold's career. An Australian umpire by the name of Phillips no-balled Mold for 'throwing' at Trent Bridge in the game against Nottinghamshire. Mold did play on for the rest of the season. But it had become clear that the action of many bowlers had become questionable. During the close season, the county captains met to discuss the question of unfair bowling. Arthur Mold was one of the bowlers whom the county captains decided not to use.

Yet none of the players on the county circuit thought Mold's action to be unfair. None other that the great W.G. Grace had said he thought Mold, "the fairest of fast bowlers".

Throughout this controversy, Mold showed considerably dignity. It is a pity that the doubt about the legality of Mold's bowling stopped him at the beginning of his career. However, it cannot be denied that Mold's twelve seasons at Old Trafford were great ones.

As Mold's figures show, he averaged nearly six wickets a match, the greatest as yet of any Lancashire bowler.

Cecil Parkin

Birthplace: Eaglescliffe
Born: 18th February 1886
Died: 15th June 1943
Played: 1914–1926

Averages in all first-class Lancashire matches

Matches	Innings	Not Outs	Runs	Highest Score	Average	100s	50s
157	189	27	1,959	57	12.09	—	4

Runs	Wickets	Average	Best	5 Wickets	10 Wickets
14,526	901	16.12	9	85	26

Number of Test Appearances – 10

POTENTIALLY, Cecil Parkin was one of the greatest bowlers in the game. He could do almost anything with a cricket ball – this was at once, both his strength and his weakness. He was a conjuror both on and off the field and the rabbits he brought out of the hat sometimes embarrassed his own side as much as his opponents.

Parkin would try anything with the ball, not once but continually – therefore it would be difficult to set a field for a bowler who could bowl a googly one ball and a donkey drop next!

If he had concentrated on being just a fast-medium bowler, he may well have been more successful than he was, but with Parkin experiment was inseparable from his temperament.

He would practise his spinners on his long-suffering wife who often ended

these sessions in tears and with her finger nails black and blue. She stuck determinedly to her role as dummy batsman and Parkin would often say in later years that it was due to his wife's encouragement that he became the bowler he was.

One trouble with Parkin was that you could never be sure when he was serious and when he was joking, for he was an inveterate leg-puller. He was the Ray East of latter-day cricket.

He first played for Lancashire in 1914, after he had spent a short-time as professional for Church in the Lancashire League. In his first match at Aigburth against Leicestershire, he took 14–99. Unhappily, the outbreak of World War One shackled Parkin's early promise.

It wasn't until 1922 that Parkin was able to play regularly for the county side. However, in 1919 he gained success against Yorkshire, taking 14 wickets in the match as a result of his bewildering change of flight, pace and spin. He also toured Australia in the winter of 1920–21 when England lost all five test matches. Parkin looked the best of the bowlers, taking many wickets but at a considerable cost. He complained that Skipper J. W. H. T. Douglas instructed him to bowl outside the off-stump and not to 'experiment' Australian cricketers and cricket writers thought Parkin was a better bowler than his figures suggested.

In the 1921 home series against the Australians, he took 16 wickets at a cost of 26.25 each, including 5–38 in the Old Trafford test. It was in this test that he and Richard Barlow opened both the batting and the bowling (the difference being, Barlow was actually chosen to do so!) At Edgbaston in 1924, he criticised his captain, Arthur Gilligan, in the press and was dropped from the side.

Parkin had a delightful action; lively, loose-limbed and with the arm held high, his follow through was full and straight.

The crowds loved Parkin and his antics. He had a devil-may-care attitude to the game and this promised excitement and pleasure. Exhibitionism was part of Parkin. When he found the crowd liked it and expected it, he fostered it! He could talk as well as he bowled (well almost!) and could conjure the ball from his pocket or flick it from his toe to his head. Parkin was a likeable man, full of energy and full of schemes for bringing about the downfall of a batsman. When talking of Cecil Parkin, it is so easy to be side-tracked from the essentials, but at his best he really was a very fine bowler.

Parkin was really a much better batsman than he cared to admit. An innings from Parkin was an hilarious sight and if Dick Tyldesley happened to be at the other end, they would beat all other professional comedy twosome you could think of!

In his later years, he was licensee at an Old Trafford hostelry and would at the end of a day's play entertain his customers with endless cricket stories.

When he died in 1943, at his request, his ashes were thrown over the Old Trafford wicket. A distinguished gathering paid their respects to a player who had both delighted and irritated them!

Eddie Paynter

Birthplace:	Oswaldtwistle
Born:	5th November 1901
Died:	5th February 1979
Played:	1926–1945

Averages in all first-class Lancashire matches

Matches	Innings	Not Outs	Runs	Highest Score	Average	100s	50s
293	445	47	16,555	322	41.59	36	79

Runs	Wickets	Average	Best	5 Wickets	10 Wickets
1,250	24	52.08	3–13	—	—

Number of Test Appearances – 20

EDDIE PAYNTER spent ten years on the ground staff before his real chance came. During those ten years he was, on occasions, brought into the county side to fill gaps, but there was no regular spot for him. Eddie Paynter was 28 years old before he played that first game. The tragedy for him was that not only did he lose seasons at the beginning of his career, but six at the end, due to the war. Therefore, his first-class career was compressed into ten seasons only.

Whilst it could be asked how such a player could be kept out of the county side for so long, it must be remembered that Ernest Tyldesley, Watson, Hallows, Makepeace and Iddon were the first five batsmen at that time.

Whilst he scored 16,555 runs at 41.59 for Lancashire, he scored 1,540 runs for England at an average of 59. Yet his average against the Australians stands at a remarkable 84.42, only bettered by Don Bradman in these epic confrontations.

Paynter made his test debut in the 'Body-line' tour of the 1932–33 series. He shot to prominence in the Brisbane Test for which his name will always

be remembered. Paynter was taken ill and sent to hospital with tonsilitis, but when England were 216–6 in reply to Australia's 340, he left his sick bed to play a gutsy and historic innings of resistance, making 83. Typically, Paynter returned in the second innings to hit the winning runs, a six. It won England the match and decided the series in England's favour. His reward in the next test, demotion to number eight!

In the 1938 home series against Australia, when Sir Len Hutton made 364 at the Oval, Eddie Paynter, like Hutton, ended the series with an average of over 100. At Trent Bridge Paynter scored 216 not out. At Lord's, Paynter scored 99 in the first innings and a stubborn 43 in the second, showing there was no better man in a crisis. When Australia batted, wicket-keeper Les Ames injured a finger and who should volunteer to don the gloves but Eddie Paynter. He conceded only five byes and also caught the Australian wicket-keeper, Barnett.

Paynter toured South Africa in 1938–39 and scored 36 hundreds, including 4 double-hundreds and a treble. His highest score of 322 was made against Sussex at Brighton.

'Roses' matches always brought the best out of Eddie Paynter. A bad ball to him was a bad ball, whether it was bowled at Old Trafford, Headingley or Aigburth. Most of Paynter's finest and enterprising knocks were played on difficult wickets. In 1932, on such a wicket and with Verity bowling at his best, he produced a superb knock of 152 out of Lancashire's 263. It enabled Lancashire to reverse the position they had been in earlier and they went on to win by an innings.

In his youth, he lost two fingers in an accident, but he was still a superb outfielder, both catcher and thrower. He would cut off certain boundaries and hurl the ball with extreme accuracy into the wicket-keeper's gloves.

Eddie Paynter was a small man, but he never once considered his lack of inches a disadvantage. He possessed a keen eye and nimble footwork. He could play every stroke in the book and many more that weren't in it! Whilst he was renowned for his driving and hooking, the shot that brought him many runs was the stroke played wide of gully, something between a cut and a slash, that sent the ball racing to the boundary.

After the war, Eddie Paynter was seen no-more in first-class cricket and moved to the Bradford League to see out his playing days.

Eddie Paynter was a loyal, professional and undervalued batsman – a man of courage and resolution. No player relished a fight more than Eddie Paynter.

Harry Pilling

Birthplace:	Ashton-under-Lyne
Born:	23rd February 1943
Died:	—
Played:	1962–1980

Averages in all first-class Lancashire matches

Matches	Innings	Not Outs	Runs	Highest Score	Average	100s	50s
323	525	65	14,841	149*	32.26	25	76

Runs	Wickets	Average	Best	5 Wickets	10 Wickets
195	1	195.00	1-42	—	—

Number of Test Appearances – 0

HARRY PILLING came straight from school to Lancashire at the tender age of 14 and he wasn't much bigger than the wickets! He arrived as a bowler and could bowl a useful leg-break.

Like most of Lancashire's cricketing greats, he had to come up the hard way. He had to fight for everything he collected as a schoolboy and, really, it was the same in first-class cricket.

Each season his target was 1,000 runs and seldom did he fail to reach it. Built like a flyweight boxer rather than a prolific run-making batsman, his lack of inches made no difference to his contribution to the Red Rose cause. He scored 14,841 runs at an average of 32.26, his highest score being 149 not out against Glamorgan at Liverpool.

He was particularly strong on the on-side and quick between the wickets. Pilling will probably always be remembered as the 'Little Giant', a batsman

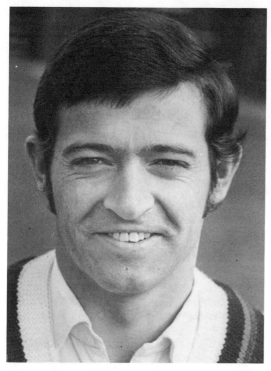

of immense quality and tremendous courage. His mid-wicket conferences with Clive Lloyd were one of the funniest sights on a cricket field. Because of the obvious difference in size between the two men, bowlers found it difficult to maintain their line and length when they were playing together. Harry enjoyed batting with Clive but was not too sure, apparently, about running with him – he claimed to be frightened of being trampled underfoot!

Pilling could slaughter the best bowlers in the country, fast and slow alike. On the field, he was a magnificent trier and his failure to win an England cap was a slight on the Test selectors rather than any reflection on his prowess.

During the close season, Harry Pilling had many jobs. These included apprentice butcher, coalman, toolmaker and a coffin representative!

It would, I feel, be difficult to find another player who has given greater service to the cause of Lancashire on the cricket field. A very popular player, the Lancashire crowds loved nothing better than this 'Little Atom' who could always produce the goods!

Winston Place

Birthplace:	Rawtenstall
Born:	7th December 1914
Died:	—
Played:	1937–1955

Averages in all first-class Lancashire matches

Matches	Innings	Not Outs	Runs	Highest Score	Average	100s	50s
298	441	43	14,605	266*	36.69	34	67

Runs	Wickets	Average	Best	5 Wickets	10 Wickets
42	1	42.00	1–2	—	—

Number of Test Appearances – 3

WINSTON PLACE was born in Rawtenstall and played the game at school. It was a natural step from the school eleven to the town second eleven.

Steady unspectacular progress brought its reward – an engagement with the county in 1936. Within a year he made his debut and was soon taking a century off the Nottinghamshire attack in which Harold Larwood and Bill Voce were the two opening bowlers.

In 1939, he took 164 off the touring West Indies. The war followed and Place, an engineer by trade, resumed his work, but he kept his 'eye-in' until he could resume his position as Lancashire's opening batsman. Place was, without doubt, the perfect foil for his opening partner Cyril Washbrook.

Winston Place was a very dependable right-handed batsman. Whilst he showed strong defence against the turning ball, he could also pull, loft the ball over the bowler's head or produce the classic cover-drive. His career took a turn for the better in 1946 when he opened with Washbrook. Prior to the Second World War, despite the odd flashes, he had been no more than an ordinary batsman.

He only represented England on three occasions, but did score 107 against the West Indies in the 1947–48 tour at Kingston. Surely Winston Place should have made more appearances at international level.

He topped 1,000 runs in eight seasons, his best being 1947, when he scored 2,501 runs at an average of 62.52.

Place derived from the game as much pleasure as he gave it. He developed a super personality – humerous, equable and modest.

My friend and teaching colleague, Peter Stafford (ex-Bolton League Secretary), to whom I am indebted for his assistance with research, tells me that when he was a boy Winston Place was his and many other young Lancashire supporters' favourite player.

Dick Pollard

Birthplace:	Westhoughton	
Born:	19th June 1912	
Died:	—	
Played:	1933–1950	

Averages in all first-class Lancashire matches

Matches	Innings	Not Outs	Runs	Highest Score	Average	100s	50s
266	298	52	3,273	63	13.30	—	7

Runs	Wickets	Average	Best	5 Wickets	10 Wickets
22,492	1,015	22.15	8–33	55	10

Number of Test Appearances – 4

IT WAS in the late 1920s that Dick Pollard from Westhoughton was talked about as a fast bowler of more than average skill and a batsman who could both defend and hit fiercely. At the age of nineteen, he was considered good enough for the County First XI, and he made his debut in the same year he became a professional.

There followed four years in club and minor county cricket. It was during this time that Pollard learned to mix his swing with length and developed the stamina which was to be his trademark in the years ahead. Like many other Lancashire Cricketing Greats, the war took a large chunk from his cricketing career. I suppose that, if the war hadn't happened, Dick Pollard would have challenged the superb bowling records of Johnny Briggs and Brian Statham.

In 1936, he took 100 wickets for the first time and repeated this achievement every season until his retirement from the first-class scene in 1950. The only exception was 1946, when he was still serving with the services and missed quite a few matches. Also in 1936, he was given a place in the Rest of England side that battled with the then county champions, Yorkshire.

Pollard was a great-hearted fast-medium bowler who would toil endlessly through the heat and burden of the day. In fact, the longer he bowled, the faster he seemed to bowl! He had a long pounding run, putting everything into his final action. His action wasn't perfect, his body being too square to

the batsman and little rhythm in his run. Yet he had so many good qualities. He attacked the wicket, bowled to his field, thrived on work and bowled a late out-swinger that was his best ball.

He had the nickname of th'owd chain horse. The title was not bestowed lightly – 'owd chain horses do not complain, neither did Dick Pollard.

The war was also largely to blame for Pollard's late introduction to Test cricket. His first appearance was in 1946 at Old Trafford against India. Pollard took 5–24 in 27 overs in India's first innings. He was chosen to tour Australasia the following winter but didn't make an appearance in Australia and only one in New Zealand. Even the great Sir Don Bradman found Pollard's omission very strange. His test record of fifteen wickets in four tests wasn't a true reflection of Pollard's ability. Pollard had great potential. Unfortunately it wasn't recognised by Dick himself or the selectors.

Without doubt, his best season was 1947 when he took 137 wickets for Lancashire. His match record was 14–216 against Middlesex at Old Trafford in 1946. Three times in his career, he took eight wickets in an innings and on two occasions, he performed the hat-trick (against Glamorgan at Preston in 1939 and against Warwickshire at Blackpool in 1947).

Red Rose fanatics will always remember Dick Pollard as one of the greatest triers who ever played for the county. He was one of a very select band of bowlers who have taken over a thousand wickets for Lancashire – it was probably sufficient reward for th'owd chain horse!

Geoff Pullar

Birthplace:	Swinton
Born:	1st August 1935
Died:	—
Played:	1954–1968

Averages in all first-class Lancashire matches

Matches	Innings	Not Outs	Runs	Highest Score	Average	100s	50s
312	524	45	16,853	176*	35.18	32	88

Runs	Wickets	Average	Best	5 Wickets	10 Wickets
305	8	38.12	3-91	—	—

Number of Test Appearances – 28

GEOFF PULLAR was born in Swinton, just three miles from the Old Trafford ground he was later to grace for 15 seasons. His early cricket was played in the Lancashire League for Werneth, where he made a great impression as a stroke-player.

He made his Lancashire debut in 1954, as an 18 year old amateur, batting in the middle order. In 1959, he was chosen to open the innings for England and went on to hit 75 in his opening international match against India.

'Noddy' Pullar was a strong left-handed batsman. He acquired his nickname because of his ability to fall asleep in almost any situation. But once he got to the middle, he was certainly awake.

He scored heavily, mainly off the front foot and accumulated plenty of runs, largely by means of the leg glance played to the ball pitching outside leg stump which he 'picked' well. His main powers were his patience, concentration and his temperamental soundness.

Geoff Pullar holds a unique record among all Lancashire's talented batsmen who have played for England in Test Matches on their home ground of Old Trafford. He is the only player to have scored a century, 131 against India – in only his second game for England. Pullar's highest score in the Test arena was in 1960 when he made a massive 175 at the Oval against South Africa.

In his career with Lancashire, Pullar scored a total of 16,853 runs at a very

healthy average of 35.18. After his days with Lancashire, he represented
Gloucestershire for two seasons.

Vernon Royle

Birthplace:	Brooklands
Born:	29th January 1854
Died:	21st May 1929
Played:	1873–1891

Averages in all first-class Lancashire matches

Matches	Innings	Not Outs	Runs	Highest Score	Average	100s	50s
74	120	8	1,754	81	15.66	—	6

Runs	Wickets	Average	Best	5 Wickets	10 Wickets
114	2	57.00	1–22	—	—

Number of Test Appearances – 1

LIKE QUITE a few of Lancashire's cricketing greats, Vernon Royle attended the Rossall School. There, at an early age, he showed the speed which was to be his greatest asset; in those early days he won the 100 yards race in 1872.

He made his Lancashire debut in 1873, whilst he was still at Rossall and, two years laters, he went on to obtain an Oxford 'blue'.

The highest innings of Royle's life was 205 for the Gentlemen of Cheshire against the Staffordshire Borderers at Chelford in 1874. In 1878, he found himself in second place in the Lancashire batting averages.

Royle was always a fast run-getter when he was well set. He would get over the ball with good style, often hitting with plenty of power.

He is one of the few first-class players who have merited lasting fame for their fielding alone. The Reverend Vernon Royle (he later went on to become a headmaster) was probably one of the world's greatest cover-points.

Royle was ambidextrous and the speed and anticipation of his movements, his superb pick-up and throw and the regularity with which he hit the wickets from impossible angles, made even the speediest of batsmen loathe to take a quick single.

He was married and had four sons, one of whom, J. S. Royle, was in the Harrow XIs of 1906 and 1907. For a short period, he was headmaster at Elstree and, in 1907, he became headmaster at Stanmore Park Preparatory School, Middlesex. It was here that he died, after a short illness, aged 75.

John Sharp

Birthplace: Hereford
Born: 15th February 1878
Died: 28th January 1938
Played: 1899–1925

Averages in all first-class Lancashire matches

Matches	Innings	Not Outs	Runs	Highest Score	Average	100s	50s
518	776	70	22,015	211	31.18	36	113

Runs	Wickets	Average	Best	5 Wickets	10 Wickets
11,821	434	27.23	9-77	18	3

Number of Test Appearances – 3

JACK SHARP showed exceptional batting ability when only 14 years of age, by scoring an amazing unbeaten 208 against Ledbury, when he lived in Herefordshire. When Sharp came into the Lancashire side, he actually came in as a fast bowler, but then reverted to his earlier penchant by becoming one of the most successful batsmen in the club's history. He went on to represent England in both capacities, performing extremely capably.

He was classed as an all-rounder of immense ability, a free-scoring right-handed batsman and a good fast-medium bowler, plus a brilliant field at cover-point. He exceeded 1,000 runs on ten occasions and in 1901, he took

112 wickets at 22.43 each and scored 883 runs and was recognised as the one notable all-rounder in the county XI. His outstanding performances with the ball include 9–77 against Worcestershire, 7–25 against Middlesex and 5–14 against Derbyshire. His batting figures are much more impressive, scoring over 20,000 runs, including his highest score of 211 against Leicestershire at Old Trafford.

He represented England on three occasions, scoring a century and taking three good wickets on his debut against the Australians.

His sporting career was unique. He won international caps at soccer and played in an F.A. Cup Final for Everton, for whom he later became a director. However, cricket was his major sport and people would come miles to watch this fast bowler whose batting combined great hitting power with soundness.

In 1925 at Old Trafford, when Lancashire were playing Middlesex in Cecil Parkin's benefit match, Sharp, who was such a brilliant fielder, put down Middlesex's opening bat Lee off the first ball of the match. The openers then went on to score 121 for the first wicket and the crowd got on to Sharp. He was greatly upset by the crowd's reaction and threatened never to play for the county again. The Lancashire Committee persuaded him to change his decision, but at the end of the season, Sharp sent in his resignation.

On his retirement, he was appointed a Test Selector and later, when the hatchets were buried, he became an honorary life-member of the Lancashire Club.

Ken Shuttleworth

Birthplace:	St Helens
Born:	13th November 1944
Died:	—
Played:	1964–1975

Averages in all first-class Lancashire matches

Matches	Innings	Not Outs	Runs	Highest Score	Average	100s	50s
177	179	62	1,929	71	16.48	—	3

Runs	Wickets	Average	Best	5 Wickets	10 Wickets
11,097	484	22.92	7–41	17	1

Number of Test Appearances – 5.

KEN SHUTTLEWORTH started playing league cricket with Earlstown at the age of 14. He moved to St Helens Recs at 17 and played ten games for the County Second XI in 1963.

He made his Lancashire debut in 1964 in the Old Trafford 'Roses' game

against Yorkshire. He only took one wicket, that of Geoffrey Boycott! He took a good few years to establish himself as a regular first-teamer.

Ken Shuttleworth was a well-built right-handed fast bowler with an action similar to Fred Trueman's. Injuries played a major role in Shuttleworth's career but, at his peak, he possessed a very quick delivery with a dangerous outswing. His best figures for the county were 7–41 against Essex at Leyton and, even in the one-day game, he showed his worth. His best figures in the John Player League were the highly creditable 5–13 against Nottinghamshire at Trent Bridge. Added to his talents as a bowler, he was also perfectly capable of holding his own with the bat, once making 71, against Gloucester-shire at Cheltenham.

In 1970, he played for England in the unofficial Test against the Rest of the World. The following winter, he toured Australia and New Zealand and was in important member of the successful Ashes-winning squad. His best performance was when he took 5–47 at the Gabba in Brisbane.

Eventually, Lancashire lost patience with his run of ailments and, though he was granted a joint testimonial with John Sullivan in 1975, he was allowed to end his career with some good performances at Leicestershire.

Jack Simmons

Birthplace:	Clayton-le-Moors
Born:	28th March 1941
Died:	—
Played:	1968–

Averages in all first-class Lancashire matches

Matches	Innings	Not Outs	Runs	Highest Score	Average	100s	50s
417	517	136	8,681	112	22.78	5	38

Runs	Wickets	Average	Best	5 Wickets	10 Wickets
25,958	974	26.65	7–64	40	6

Number of Test Appearances – 0

JACK SIMMONS played for Enfield as an amateur until he was 19. He then turned professional with Baxenden in the Ribblesdale League. He spent four years with Baxenden, followed by three with Barnoldswick. A year with Blackpool in the Northern League was his final league contract.

He came into the Lancashire first team in 1968 at the ripe old age of 27! Oddly enough it was at Blackpool that he made his debut against Northamptonshire.

His first century in the first-class game came against Sussex in 1971. He was sent in as a nightwatchman to play the last five deliveries. He lasted just over three hours to score 112, including 21 fours. Later that season, at the age of 30, he was awarded his county cap.

'Flat' Jack is a fine, strong and courageous batsman, an excellent catcher and a safe fielder and one of the most successful slow bowlers, especially in one-day cricket. In fact, Jack soon provided stability and produced superb cricket with both bat and ball. Jack is loved by so many cricket fans, not just Lancastrians, but world-wide.

In 1971, Jack went to the island of Tasmania when, in terms of cricket, the island was a 'nobody.' By the time Jack had finished with Tasmanian cricket, the side was well respected world-wide and winners of the Gillette Cup. Jack first found his way into the hearts of the Tasmanians by hitting the winning runs off the last ball in a Gillette Cup victory over Victoria – it was the island's first success in the competition in five years of trying. Jack also launched his own personal campaign to get Tasmania accepted into Sheffield Shield cricket. In 1977, he achieved this aim.

The 1978–79 season that Jack spent 'Down Under' was a huge success. He took 7–59 against Queensland and in the Gillette Cup Final, he hit an unbeaten 55, took 4–17 and won the Man of the Match award!

Jack is a great club man and a wonderful coach. He has never missed signing an autograph yet, and is my son's favourite player.

During the Old Trafford game between Lancashire and the touring Australians in June 1989, Simmons, no longer assured of an automatic first-team place, announced that he would be retiring at the end of the season, prompting the following tribute from chairman, Bob Bennett: "We are sad that an era in Lancashire cricket will come to an end in September.

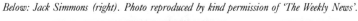

Below: Jack Simmons (right). Photo reproduced by kind permission of 'The Weekly News'.

Reg Spooner

Birthplace:	Litherland
Born:	21st October 1880
Died:	2nd October 1961
Played:	1899–1921

Averages in all first-class Lancashire matches

Matches	Innings	Not Outs	Runs	Highest Score	Average	100s	50s
170	280	14	9,889	247	37.17	25	35

Runs	Wickets	Average	Best	5 Wickets	10 Wickets
554	5	110.80	1–5	—	—

Number of Test Appearances – 10

REGINALD HERBERT SPOONER attended Marlborough School and was regarded as the school's finest batsman. In his last year there, he scored 926 runs at an average of 71.00, whilst at the same time topping the batting averages.

He made his Lancashire debut in 1899 against Middlesex at Lord's. At this time, he was also in his final year at Marlborough. He'd already scored 198 against the arch enemy, Rugby School. Records state that he treated the Middlesex opening bowlers, J.T. Hearne and Albert Trott with the same disdain he'd shown to bowlers he'd encountered whilst playing for Marlborough. He scored 44 in the first innings and 83 in the second – he had arrived!

Even though he had now left school, he was still unable to play for Lancashire, as he posted with the militia to Ireland. He

then served in the Boer War in South Africa and so it was in 1903 when he finally played cricket again in England. Yet his business commitments restricted the time Spooner was able to devote to cricket and only in six seasons did he play on a regular basis.

It has been said many times that Spooner was primarily a fast-wicket batsman and that he wasn't so effective against the ball that deviated as it came to the bat. Yet Spooner was one of the few early batsmen to read and play the googly with confidence. Spooner's batting appeared so effortless that only the fieldmen trying to cut off one of his drives or vainly chasing it to the boundary fence, realised the tremendous power he generated.

In 1910, in the Roses encounter at Old Trafford, Spooner scored 200 not out. It still stands as the highest score made by a Lancashire player in the Battle of the Roses. Spooner was brilliant on that day. Sir Neville Cardus, who witnessed his performance, was moved to write he "changed Old Trafford's turf into textures of silk or gold." Yorkshires bowlers could do nothing to halt the flow of runs and their captain couldn't set a field to contain him.

Spooner first played for England in the fourth test of the 1905 series, at Old Trafford against Australia. He scored 52 in that match and the Aussies were defeated by an innings. He scored 119 against South Africa at Lords in 1912. In his ten test matches, he scored 481 runs at an average of 32. It seems such a pity that he took little part in the international arena, when he obviously had so much to give.

Spooner represented the Gentlemen several times in their fixtures against the Players. His innings of 114 in 1906 at Lord's, still ranks as one of the finest played in these encounters.

Wisden describing it said "Spooner played one of the finest innings of his life. Better batting was not seen at Lord's all the season. Powerful on-driving and very skilful play on the leg-side were the features of his innings."

Spooner's figures do not conjure up the brilliance of his stroke-play, or the immense pleasure it brought to the thousands of Red Rose supporters.

As a fieldsman, Spooner was rated as one of the greatest cover fielders in the game. For Lancashire, he was compared to the great Vernon Royle, and that is praise indeed.

In fact, everything that Reg Spooner did out in the middle was a model of ease and grace, but as all followers of Lancashire will know, his particular glory was the off-drive. Spooner's drive began as an orthodox stroke, but at the last second, he gave it individuality by a flick of the wrists. The charm of Spooner's cricket was a true reflection of the man himself – friendly, modest and sincere.

Brian Statham

Birthplace:	Gorton, Manchester
Born:	17th June 1930
Died:	—
Played:	1950–1968

Averages in all first-class Lancashire matches

Matches	Innings	Not Outs	Runs	Highest Score	Average	100s	50s
430	501	98	4,237	62	10.51	—	5

Runs	Wickets	Average	Best	5 Wickets	10 Wickets
27,470	1,816	15.12	8-34	109	10

Number of Test Appearances – 70

BRIAN OR 'GEORGE' STATHAM became a cricketer almost by accident! As a young boy, his sporting interests lay with soccer and tennis, certainly not cricket.

After leaving school, he served with the R.A.F. and turned to cricket, only because of the lack of opportunity to play tennis. The secretary of his unit team was impressed by his bowling and wrote to Old Trafford asking them to give Statham a trial. On the day of the trial, it rained very heavily and he didn't even bother to turn up. Lancashire had not forgotten, though, and invited him back the following spring. He performed satisfactorily and, two weeks after he was demobbed, he joined the ground staff.

He made his county debut in 1950, impressing with his accuracy and speed. He ended that season with 37 wickets from 300 overs at a cost of 16.56 each, including 5-52 in his first 'Roses' encounter.

The following winter, England were in Australia and hard-hit by injuries, Statham, along with Tattersall, was called out as a replacement. He made his test debut later in the tour in New Zealand.

In 1951, he played his first full season in the County Championship and ended up taking 97 wickets at 15 runs each. He also topped the county bowling averages. He was quite content to bowl fast and straight, moving the ball off the seam both ways. He worked on the theory that if the batsman missed, he generally hit.

He continued to represent England regularly in both home series and tours abroad. In the early 1950s he visited India, Pakistan and the West Indies, taking wickets with great regularity. It was in 1954–55 in the Ashes confrontation that Statham teamed up with Frank 'Typhoon' Tyson to give England their fastest opening attack. Statham often bowled into the wind, his accuracy and control the ideal complement to Tyson's pace.

In 1955, against the South African's at Lord's, Statham bowled magnificently to take 7–39. He continued to play regularly for England, and in 70 matches he took 252 wickets. His last appearance for his country was in 1965 at the age of 35 when he took 7 South African wickets for 145 runs – proving he was still a force to be reckoned with on the Test scene.

On thirteen occasions he took more than a 100 wickets in a season. He took 15 for 89 against Warwickshire in 1957 and seven years later took 15 for 108 against Leicestershire. He performed the hat-trick three times.

Statham captained Lancashire for three seasons, 1965–67. They were difficult years; senior experienced players had left the club and there was a great influx of young new blood. He knew the captaincy would be difficult, but it was a challenge and there was never any question of him refusing the Committee's offer.

The way he left the first-class scene was typical of the man. A commercial opportunity arose and so he gave the Lancashire Committee plenty of notice of his future intentions, resigning the captaincy at the end of the 1967 season. He had intended to go at the end of June 1968, but he delayed the move so he could play in one more Roses match. It was August 1968, a match I remember vividly. Lancashire had batted first making a modest total. Statham along with Ken Higgs shot out Yorkshire batsmen as though there was no tomorrow. Overnight, Yorkshire were 34–8 (Statham 5–20) and though they recovered somewhat the following morning, Statham still had figures of 6–34. After his retirement, he had offers from League clubs, but he turned them all down.

Brian Statham was a superb bowler, both fast and accurate. Fittingly, he was awarded the C.B.E. for his services to cricket.

Allan Steel

Birthplace:	Liverpool
Born:	24th September, 1858
Died:	15th June 1914
Played:	1877-1893

Averages in all first-class Lancashire matches

Matches	Innings	Not Outs	Runs	Highest Score	Average	100s	50s
47	72	5	1,960	105	29.95	1	13

Runs	Wickets	Average	Best	5 Wickets	10 Wickets
3,134	238	13.16	9-63	26	7

Number of Test Appearances – 13

ALLAN GIBSON STEEL was one of the greatest of all Marlborough cricketers. He was in the College XI from 1874 until 1877 and was captain in his last two years. He was also a key member of the great Cambridge University XIs of 1878, 1879, 1880 (as captain) and 1881. Steel was also a first choice for the Gentlemen in their fixture against the Players.

He didn't captain Lancashire very often – more the loss, apparently, for Lancashire, for Steel holds quite a remarkable record as a captain. He led Marlborough to victory over Rugby, he led Cambridge when they won against Oxford, he captained the Gentlemen against the Players and won, led Lancashire against Yorkshire to victory and, finally, was at the helm when England beat Australia! Steel was even reckoned by some in his day to be the greatest amateur all-rounder after W. G. Grace.

He was a quick-footed batsman, a superb driver of the ball on both sides of the wicket. He was an accurate right-arm slow bowler, too, spinning the ball either way whilst keeping a full length.

Steel was very successful in 1878, his first full season in first-class cricket, taking 164 wickets at 9.43 and scoring 537 runs at an average of 22.37. It was, without doubt, the best season of his career, though he did take 130 wickets in 1881 at an average of 13.41. His best bowling was against Yorkshire in 1878 at Old Trafford, when he took 9 wickets for 63.

He represented England on thirteen occasions, all against Australia, nine at home and four 'Down Under'. He was captain in 1886 when England won all three matches and again in 1888, when the bowling of Ferris and Turner won the game for Australia.

He scored two Test hundreds, 148 at Lord's in 1884 and 135 not out at Sydney a year earlier. For England, Steel scored 600 runs at an average of 35.29 and took 29 wicket at a cost of 20.86 each. In all his first-class matches, he scored 6,759 runs, including seven centuries, and took a total of 781 wickets. Of those, some 238 came when he was playing for Lancashire. In all, Steel only played 47 matches for the Red Rose county, but his fugures during that period surely place him among the great players. At an average of just 13.16, Steel took ten wickets on no fewer than seven occasions and took five twenty-six times!

Steel played his final first-class match against I Zingari in 1895.

Roy Tattersall

	Birthplace:	Bolton
	Born:	17th August 1922
	Died:	—
	Played:	1948–1960

Averages in all first-class Lancashire matches

Matches	Innings	Not Outs	Runs	Highest Score	Average	100s	50s
277	312	128	1,786	58	9.70	—	1

Runs	Wickets	Average	Best	5 Wickets	10 Wickets
20,316	1,168	17.39	9–40	83	16

Number of Test Appearances – 16

ROY TATTERSALL came into the first-class game relatively late. It was in 1948 at the age of 26 that he played his first game for Lancashire. It was another two years before he was awarded his county cap.

Roy Tattersall was a right-arm off-break bowler. He was a first-rate exponent of accuracy, also being able to vary his pace. Without doubt, 1950 was his year. He headed the national averages, taking more wickets (193 at 13.59 each) than any other bowler in first-class cricket. As is perhaps the norm, anybody from north of Watford Gap, no matter how well they perform, finds it difficult to break into the test team – this was the case with Roy Tattersall, despite his brilliant season. He wasn't chosen for any of the test matches that summer. He wasn't chosen originally either for the winter tour of Australia. However, the M.C.C. team was plagued by injuries, so both Tattersall and Brian Statham were flown out to strengthen England's depleted squad.

Between 1951–1954, he played in 16 Tests, taking 58 wickets at 26 runs each, but the rise to prominence of Jim Laker put paid to any future international appearances for England. In 1951 at Lord's against South Africa, he took 7–52 on a rain affected wicket in the first innings and followed it up with 5–49 in the second. In the 1951–1952 tour to India, he bowled very economically and at Kanpur on a helpful wicket, he helped himself to 8–125.

For the Red-Rose, he continued to baffle the oppostion. Six times he took eight or more wickets in an innings and took one hundred wickets or more in a season on eight occasions. At Old Trafford in 1953 against Nottinghamshire he had the match analysis of 14–73, including a 'hat-trick'. In 1956, he completely devastated Yorkshire. He took 6–47 in their first inning and 8–43 in the second. In 1958, the batsmen began to 'read' him better and so he wasn't as successful in his latter years.

Roy Tattersall was the Lancashire Number 11. His batting technique brought much fun to the Old Trafford faithful. Tattersall had no illusions about his method. He would ensure that his back foot was firmly inside the crease and then dart forward towards the pitch of the ball – more in hope than judgement!

A good-humoured, cheerful man, Tattersall was a highly popular player at Old Trafford. Known affectionately as 'Tatt', he was sorely missed when he called it a day.

Ernest Tyldesley

Birthplace:	Roe Green
Born:	5th February 1889
Died:	5th May 1962
Played:	1909–1936

Averages in all first-class Lancashire matches

Matches	Innings	Not Outs	Runs	Highest Score	Average	100s	50s
573	850	93	34,222	256*	45.20	90	166

Runs	Wickets	Average	Best	5 Wickets	10 Wickets
332	6	55.33	3-33	—	—

Number of Test Appearances – 14

ERNEST TYLDESLEY played his first game for Lancashire in 1909 against Warwickshire at Aigburth, scoring 61. Despite Ernest scoring more runs in his career than any other Lancashire batsman, he was slower to develop than older brother Johnny. In 1913, he hit the headlines by scoring three centuries in the space of one week in the month of June.

It was not until after the war, however, that the full range of Ernest's batting ability flourished. His greatest strength was on the on-side. His hooking was superb and his driving and turning to fine-leg elegant.

Ernest was often an uncertain starter, but once he got the 'feel' of the wicket and was well set, he could score very quickly, using his full repertoire.

He played in 14 Tests and perhaps

didn't represent his country as often as his ability warranted. In fact, a legend has grown up which suggests that Ernest never lived up to his reputation in Test matches. Yet, in these 14 appearances, he scored 990 runs (including three centuries) at an average of 55.00.

Ernest made his England debut in 1921 in the unhappy First Test against Warwick Armstrong's Australians. In the second innings he was hit on the head by a ball from Gregory, knocked out and to make matters worse, the ball rolled on to his wicket! He didn't play again until the fourth test at Old Trafford and even though he top-scored with 81, he wasn't in the team for the following Test! Who says there isn't a North-South divide?

On the 1927–1928 tour of South Africa, he topped the batting averages and hit Test hundreds at Durban and Johannesburg. In 1928, he hit 122 against the West Indies at Lords and was given a place on the winter tour to Australia. There were some great players in the England side that tour and so Tyldesley had to sit out many games. It prompted M. A. Noble, the old Australiam captain to write:

> "It seems a pity that knowing this man to be a very fine batsman, the Englishmen did not persevere with him, regardless of a few early failures, until he struck form. They lost the services of a class batsman and great run-getter."

Unfortunately, he never played for England again.

For Lancashire, he hit 90 centuries, 102 in all his career, the first Lancashire man to do so. He hit 5 double-hundreds, his highest being an unbeaten 256 against Warwickshire at Old Trafford in 1930. Nineteen times he scored over 1,000 runs in a season, three times over 2,000 runs and in 1928, he scored 3,024 runs at an average of 79.57.

Probably the best innings Ernest Tyldesley played was his double-hundred at the Oval in 1923. Lancashire were in great trouble, six wickets remained and they still needed 117 runs to avoid an innings defeat. Tyldesley scored 236 in five hours and saved the game.

'Roses' matches are usually a good guide to a Lancashire batsman's value. Ernest Tyldesley scored four centuries in these games.

Tyldesley retired from active cricket in 1936 and was elected to membership of the Committee of Lancashire County Cricket Club.

In the last few months of Ernest Tyldesley's life, with his eyesight beginning to fail and a constant pain in the legs that helped him run many of those 34,222 runs, he would still shrug off his infirminty – he never gave in easily to anyone or anything!

John Tyldesley

Birthplace:	Roe Green
Born:	22nd November 1873
Died:	27th November 1943
Played:	1895–1923

Averages in all first-class Lancashire matches

Matches	Innings	Not Outs	Runs	Highest Score	Average	100s	50s
507	824	52	31,949	295*	41.38	73	157

Runs	Wickets	Average	Best	5 Wickets	10 Wickets
170	2	85.00	1–4	—	—

Number of Test Appearances – 31

JOHN THOMAS TYLDESLEY made his first team debut for Lancashire in the 1895 season against Gloucestershire at Old Trafford. He scored 33 not out in Lancashire's second innings. At Edgbaston in the following game, he scored 152 against Warwickshire. He played ten matches that summer and followed it with a full season in 1896, but a much quieter one.

In 1897, he again destroyed Warwickshire, with a century in each innings and immediately followed these scores up with 174 at Old Trafford against Sussex.

In 1898, though the county didn't have a particularly flourishing summer, Johnny Tyldesley scored almost 2,000 runs in all first-class matches. It was in this season that he hit his first double-hundred against Derbyshire at Old Trafford.

His list of hundreds include one against every county then playing the first-class game. His favourite ground must surely have been Edgbaston, because he scored no less than eleven centuries in county and representative games.

Without doubt, his best year was 1901, when J. T. scored 3,041 runs at an average of 55.29. Moreover, the majority of his runs were made on wickets which would make a lot of todays batsmen very wary indeed! At Old Trafford in the fixture against Essex, he came up against the fast bowler, C. J. Kortright. He hit Tyldesley in the face with a vicious 'bouncer'. Tyldesley retired for repairs, but after lunch he returned with his cheek heavily plastered and proceeded to savage Kortright.

In 1899, Tyldesley was called in to the England side and from then until 1909, he was an automatic choice, making thirty-one appearances.

In the 1903–04 series against Australia at Melbourne, England scored a little over 300 in their first innings, with Tyldesley top-scorer on 97. There

then followed a series of rain-storms and Australia could only make 122 in reply. When England went in for the second time, the wicket was described as 'impossible' by cricket historians. Trumble and his fellow-bowlers were making the ball come through at awkward and varying heights. England were dismissed for 103, but Tyldesley scored a superb 62. Australia were dismissed for 111, which was much higher than they imagined they would get, as England put down as many as eight chances in the field.

All Tyldesley's runs at Test-match level were made against top-class bowlers on indifferent wickets.

In the 1905 series, Tyldesley used his adroit footwork to combat the leg-side bowling approach of the fiery Armstrong. He hit 56 and 61 at Trent Bridge to enable England to clinch victory and a century at Headingley adopting the same tactics. At Old Trafford, he notched an unbeaten 112 in a drawn game.

John Tyldesley was a great batsman to watch. He had amazing speed of foot and a perfect body balance. During the close season, he would do as much ballroom dancing as possible in order to retain poise of body and nimbleness of foot. He possessed a complete range of strokes and, when playing a long innings, he used them all to good effect with plenty of power behind them There surely cannot have been a greater exponent of the square-cut. He moved across like lightning, his head over the ball, all his weight thrown into the stroke and fairly cracked it to the boundary.

In 1919 when cricket resumed after the war, Tyldesley was almost forty and only played regularly for one more season. He had been too old for active service and spent the war years organising cricket matches for war charities.

John Tyldesley was respected by everyone. He was quiet, even-tempered and unostentatious. Nevertheless, he had a steady and determined attitude to the game and to life, which was the foundation of his cricket and of his character.

Dick Tyldesley

Birthplace:	Westhoughton
Born:	11th March 1897
Died:	17th September 1943
Played:	1919–1931

Averages in all first-class Lancashire matches

Matches	Innings	Not Outs	Runs	Highest Score	Average	100s	50s
374	435	47	6,126	105	15.78	1	15

Runs	Wickets	Average	Best	5 Wickets	10 Wickets
24,139	1,449	16.65	8–15	100	22

Number of Test Appearances – 1

DICK TYLDESLEY was not a relation of Johnny or Ernest, but three members of his family had played for the county before the first World War. Dick was supposed to be a leg-break and googly bowler, but he took the majority of his wickets with a delivery that didn't break at all. His top spinner brought him a great number of wickets, many from l.b.w. decisions. He didn't turn the ball very much, just enough to beat the bat, but he was quick enough to make it hard for the batsman to get to the pitch of the ball and, on a helpful pitch, he could be quite devastating.

His greatest asset was his consistency of length, no matter how much punishment he was coming in for.

Dick Tyldesley first played for Lancashire in 1919 and in the thirteen seasons between then and 1931, he took 1449 wickets at a cost only 16.65 runs each. His aggregate of wickets, had only been passed by Briggs, Mold and Statham. For ten consecutive seasons (1922–1931) he took 100 wickets or more in a season. His best being 1924, when he took 184 wickets in all matches, 167 of these were for Lancashire. With the help of Cecil Parkin, he helped Lancashire to shoot Yorkshire out for 33. He took eleven wickets against Surrey on two occasions and twelve against the touring South Africans. When Leicestershire visited Old Trafford he took 5 wickets without conceding a run. Throughout the 1926–1930 seasons, he played a great part in helping Lancashire to the County Championship. In 1929 at

Derby, he dismissed the last two batsmen in the innings with consecutive balls and the first two batsmen in their next innings with the first two balls he delivered!

Dick Tyldesley proved irrestible in county cricket but was far less effective in the highest class. Yet, in 1930 his bowling won him a Test place against Australia at Trent Bridge. This Test call-up caused him to miss his own benefit match!

At the end of the 1931 season, he 'retired' at the age of thirty-three after a disagreement with the Old Trafford Committee.

Dick Tyldesley was a cheerful man, his batting was 'village green' and his fielding superb, taking some close to the wicket catches in breath-taking fashion, despite his ample bulk! He is remembered with great affection at Old Trafford – his rosy red countenance shining out from the pavilion photographs for all time.

Albert Ward

Birthplace:	Waterloo, Leeds
Born:	21st November 1865
Died:	6th January 1939
Played:	1889–1904

Averages in all first-class Lancashire matches

Matches	Innings	Not Outs	Runs	Highest Score	Average	100s	50s
330	554	47	15,392	185	30.96	24	78

Runs	Wickets	Average	Best	5 Wickets	10 Wickets
2,380	65	36.61	6–29	4	—

Number of Test Appearances – 7

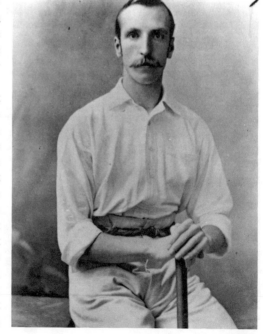

ALBERT WARD, a Yorkshireman by birth, made a few appearances for the White Rose county, but was soon poached to play for Lancashire.

Ward was an elegant right-handed opening batsman, at his best when cutting or driving. He made his debut for Lancashire in 1889 against the M.C.C. at Lord's, scoring 95. He followed this up soon afterwards with 114 not out against Middlesex, also at Lord's. At the end of his first season, he finished second in the batting averages, with 29. He went on to be a source of strength to Lancashire batting for fourteen years.

Ward was the first professional to reach a four figure aggregate for Lancashire in a season's county matches and nine times consecutively in first-class cricket he made over 1,000 runs in a season. His best year was 1895, when he scored 1,790 runs at an average of 42.

Albert Ward possessed a superb temperament and a sound defence. He was also a more than useful slow bowler and a very good fielder in the deep. As an opening batsman, he carried his bat through an innings on five occasions, the best being 140 out of 281 at Bristol against Gloucestershire in 1893. Standing just over 6 feet, he used his long reach in defence and, though careful, he cut well and drove the ball with plenty of power.

In 1899 in the match against Derbyshire at Old Trafford, Ward was dismissed in an unusual way. In playing a ball from the Derbyshire bowler, Dearden, he broke his bat, a piece of wood knocked off the leg bail and he was out for 72, 'hit-wicket'.

During his most successful season, he began to plan for his future. He opened a Sports Outfitters in Bolton and continued to work there until his death in 1939. The shop lived on for many years after the war and was the shop where I bought my first cricket bat!

Below: Cyril Washbrook

Cyril Washbrook

Birthplace: Barrow, Blackburn
Born: 6th December 1914
Died: —
Played: 1933–1959

Averages in all first-class Lancashire matches

Matches	Innings	Not Outs	Runs	Highest Score	Average	100s	50s
500	756	95	27,863	251*	42.15	58	149

Runs	Wickets	Average	Best	5 Wickets	10 Wickets
268	4	67.00	1–4	—	—

Number of Test Appearances – 37

CYRIL WASHBROOK was born at Barrow near Blackburn and spent the best part of his early years watching the local club and, in particular, Eddie Paynter.

At school, at Barrow and at Bridgnorth in Shropshire where the family moved to, Washbrook was considered a cricketing prodigy. It wasn't long before he was playing for the school first team and eventually Bridgnorth 1st XI. In his first season with Bridgnorth, he scored well over 1,000 runs.

At the age of 16, he was offered terms to join the ground staffs of both Lancashire and Warwickshire. Despite the more attractive terms offered by the Midland County, young Cyril plumped for Lancashire. (Did the fact that his one-time hero Eddie Paynter, now in Lancashire's first team, sway his decision?)

At Old Trafford, he came under the expert eye of Harry Makepeace, who ensured that Cyril had experience in the nets of all types of bowling. His first minor counties match as a member of the ground staff saw him score an unbeaten double hundred against Yorkshire. Also playing in the same game was a slightly younger Len Hutton.

Washbrook made his first-team debut in 1933 against Sussex at Old Trafford. He made 7 in the first innings batting at number 5, but when allowed to open in the second innings he scored 40. His next game was against Surrey and it brought Cyril his first hundred, 152 to be precise. In

1935, in the match against Oxford University, he scored 228 out of Lancashire's total of 431. Later that season, he carried his bat through both innings of the match against Worcestershire and was awarded his county cap. That year he scored over 1700 runs at an average of over 45. He scored over a thousand runs in 1936, but the following year after a run of indifferent scores, he was put back in the second team in an attempt to restore his lost confidence. After his first minor county 'ton' of the season, he was restored to first-team duty and responded with 72 against Leicestershire and 121 not out against Northamptonshire.

He gained a Test place, albeit as a replacement in the Oval test against New Zealand. George Duckworth advised him to look to his fielding as well as his batting. This he did and was well remembered for it in a match marred by rain. The war interrupted his progress just as he was reaching his full powers.

After the war, county cricket resumed in 1946 and Washbrook celebrated with 2,400 runs and nine hundreds and an average of 68.57 in all matches. He continued his Test career in the series against India and was nominated as one of Wisden's 'Five Cricketers of the Year'. He was chosen to go to Australia in 1946–47 and in the second innings of the third test at Melbourne scored 112, his first Test century. His opening partnerships with Hutton marked the beginning of their long association.

In the glorious summer of 1947, he scored 2,662 runs at an average of 68.25. He hit eleven hundreds that summer, including double-centuries against Surrey and Sussex. Runs flowed steadily over the next few seasons and Washbrook, whether it was with Hutton for England or Place for Lancashire, played his part in good opening stands.

Washbrook's Test career flourished. He played in four of the five Tests against Australia in 1948. He scored more runs than all the England batsmen other than Compton and averaged over 50. He toured South Africa in 1948–49 and averaged 60 for the tour. In the Second Test, he and Hutton set up a new record for first-wicket partnerships in Test matches. In 1950, injury denied him a place in the four Tests against the West Indies, but in the two he did play, he tamed both Ramadhin and Valentine and hit 114 at Lord's. He toured Australia in 1950–51 but wasn't as successful and he was never to open with Hutton again.

He was recalled to the Test arena in 1956 at the age of 42. At the time he was a Test Selector and had to leave the room when his name was suggested to strengthen the English batting at Headingley. England were 17–3 when Washbrook joined skipper May. They batted throughout the day, almost. May was out soon after reaching his hundred just before the close of play. The following day, the Yorkshire crowd were willing Washbrook to reach his hundred, but it wasn't to be – he was l.b.w. to Benaud for 98.

In all, he played in 37 Tests, scoring 2,569 runs at an average of almost 43, once again the war years depriving Lancashire and England cricket of what would surely been Washbrook's peak. In 1954 he became Lancashire's first professional captain and held the post until he retired in 1959. He then became team manager of the county side for one season. He was later on the County Cricket Committee and then a Test Selector.

He was an aggressive batsman by temperament. Primarily a back-foot player, he nevertheless drove well on the on-side. His most characteristic stroke, however, was the square-cut which he played beautifully. He was a perfectionist, always setting a high standard for himself and those who played under him.

Alec Watson

Birthplace:	Coatbridge
Born:	4th November 1844
Died:	26th October 1920
Played:	1871–1893

Averages in all first-class Lancashire matches

Matches	Innings	Not Outs	Runs	Highest Score	Average	100s	50s
283	423	88	4,187	74	12.49	—	3

Runs	Wickets	Average	Best	5 Wickets	10 Wickets
17,516	1,308	13.39	9–118	98	26

Number of Test Appearances – 0

ALEC WATSON was a Scotsman who was snapped up by the Rusholme Club in Manchester whilst touring with a team from Lanarkshire. In his early days, Watson seemed to have a reputation for being a cricket mercenary, playing for any team who were willing to pay him!

In 1871, at the age of twenty-seven, Watson made his debut for the county side. It was the beginning of a successful career, for he was a prolific member of the Red Rose attack for more than twenty years.

He was a superbly accurate off-break bowler, taking the majority of his

wickets with his most dangerous ball that kept very low after pitching. In the twenty-two years that Watson played, he took over 1300 wickets at an average of 13.39.

In 1881, Lancashire won the County Championship out-right for the first time. Like many contemporary bowlers, Watson was not exempt from accusations of throwing. In 1886 in the Lancashire fixture against the M.C.C. Watson took 6 for 8 off 15 overs, as the M.C.C. were dismissed for 30! The following year, he succeeded in passing a hundred wickets for the first time. In 1889, Watson took 90 wickets at 12.65 runs each and finished fourth in the national averages behind two of his Lancashire colleagues, Briggs and Mold. All this at the remarkable age of forty-five!

In 1891, Watson broke down with a strain and, although he returned the following season, he dropped out of the team a year later, with Johnny Briggs and Arthur Mold bearing the brunt of the bowling.

One imagines that Alec Watson took his cricket very seriously indeed. He was a very useful batsman and one of the best slip fielders of his day, but he will always be remembered for the fine bowler he was.

At the age of fifty-four, five years after he dropped out of first-class cricket, he was asked by the Lancashire Committee, because of a shortage of bowlers, to hold himself in readiness to play at the Oval against Surrey. Fortunately, he declined as Surrey notched up 634, with Tom Hayward hitting a treble hundred.

Frank Watson

Birthplace:	Nottingham
Born:	17th September 1898
Died:	1st February 1976
Played:	1920–1937

Averages in all first-class Lancashire matches

Matches	Innings	Not Outs	Runs	Highest Score	Average	100s	50s
456	644	48	22,833	300*	37.06	49	107

Runs	Wickets	Average	Best	5 Wickets	10 Wickets
12,811	402	31.86	5-31	5	—

Number of Test Appearances – 0

FRANK WATSON made his Lancashire debut in 1920. Whilst he proved his worth as a solid, reliable cricketer, both with bat and ball, there was certainly nothing flambuoyant about his cricket. In fact, because of his batting technique, he was a player that even the most ardent of Lancashire followers wished to see as little as possible of, but there can be no arguing about his value to the county!

Watson usually gave the impression that his main objective was to stay there, often he did stay there and when he did, the runs came. He could drive the overpitched ball and was a good hooker. Watson was a member of the Lancashire team during the five times they won the County Championship and a notable contributor.

His best season was 1928, when in county matches, he scored 2,403 runs at an average of 68.25, hitting 9 hundreds including 300 not out at Old Trafford against Surrey.

He never did represent England, as competition for places in those days was very strong. His representative cricket was confined to one appearance for the Players at Lord's and an occasional Test Trial.

Apart from his batting, he was a useful medium-pace bowler, bowling mainly in-swing and having the knack to break tiresome partnerships – Watson was also a good fielder, usually occupying first slip.

His career was shortened by a bad blow in the eye by a ball from Bill Bowes. His sight wasn't affected, but his confidence against the quicker bowlers was and he dropped out of the Lancashire side when he was only 37 years old.

Alan Wharton

Birthplace:	Heywood
Born:	30th April 1923
Died:	—
Played:	1946–1960

Averages in all first-class Lancashire matches

Matches	Innings	Not Outs	Runs	Highest Score	Average	100s	50s
392	589	55	17,921	199	33.55	25	94

Runs	Wickets	Average	Best	5 Wickets	10 Wickets
7,094	225	31.52	7–33	2	—

Number of Test Appearances – 1

ON HIS discharge from the Senior Service, Alan Wharton was offered and accepted a position on the staff at Old Trafford. He made his county debut in the first-team in 1946 and it was soon evident that here was a player of immense promise. He was an attacking left-handed batsman and a more than useful right-arm medium-pace bowler.

Alan Wharton had a will to succeed and a determination that he should play attractive cricket. His batting was instinctive – his courage and confidence was implicit in every bold stroke he played. In 1956 Lancashire won a Championship match without losing a wicket. Their opponents were Leicestershire (where Wharton was eventually to move to). The first day was washed out and, on the second, Leicestershire were bowled out for 108. Alan Wharton and his opening partner, Jack Dyson, scored 166 for the first wicket, at which point Geoff Eldrich, the deputy captain, declared. Leicestershire failed again, this time all out for 122, and Wharton and Dyson knocked off the requisite number of runs to win.

Wharton surpassed 1,000 runs or more in eleven seasons. His best year was 1959, when he scored 2,157 runs at an average of 40.69. His highest score of 199 was made against Sussex at Hove.

He represented his country only once, against New Zealand, not really doing himself justice. After making his reputation with Lancashire, he moved to Grace Road, where he had three prolific seasons with Leicestershire. A man of many talents, Wharton was a Rugby League Player, a Justice of the Peace and a Schoolteacher. Nowadays, he is heavily involved with Colne Cricket Club and is the League Representative for the Lancashire League.

Barry Wood

Birthplace:	Ossett
Born:	26th December 1942
Died:	—
Played:	1966–1979

Averages in all first-class Lancashire matches

Matches	Innings	Not Outs	Runs	Highest Score	Average	100s	50s
260	424	56	12,969	198	35.24	23	64

Runs	Wickets	Average	Best	5 Wickets	10 Wickets
6,910	251	27.52	7-52	8	—

Number of Test Appearances – 12

BARRY WOOD spent seven years with the White Rose county on the other side of the Pennines before joining Lancashire. He gained his pre-Yorkshire experience playing for Dewsbury, Hanging Heaton, Mirfield, Bingley and Barnsley. In 1964, he made his Yorkshire debut, but two years later, he made that most important move.

In 1968, he was awarded his county cap by Lancashire. He was a very important member of Lancashire's Gillette Cup triumphs of the 1970s. He was outstanding for Lancashire in the one-day game. He won six Gillette Man of the Match awards and eight individual awards from Benson and Hedges.

He represented England on 12 occasions. His international career started promisingly, Wood scoring 90 off the Aussies and Dennis Lillee in particular. His Test career came to a halt when he was cruelly exposed by the Indian spinners.

Barry Wood played three very important roles during his time with Lancashire. He was a very patient and correct opening batsman whose highest County Championship score was 198 against Glamorgan at Liverpool. Woody was also an excellent gully fielder and a more than useful medium bowler, who could swing the ball both ways in cloudy conditions, his best County Championship figures being 7–52. He had a successful benefit for Lancashire in 1979, later moving on to Derbyshire and then playing Minor Counties cricket with Cheshire.

Appendices
Statistical Analysis

Whilst it is purely a matter of opinion as to how good a player a man is or has been, and it is certainly true that figures seldom tell the true story of any cricketer, I hope the following will go some way to explaining why I have chosen the following eleven players as my team of 'Lancashire greats':

1. Archie MacLaren
2. Cyril Washbrook
3. Ernest Tyldesley
4. Clive Lloyd
5. Eddie Paynter
6. Johnny Tyldesley
7. Farokh Engineer
8. Johnny Briggs
9. Cecil Parkin
10. Brian Statham
11. Ted McDonald

Lancashire Top Tens

The following section lists the best performances in each of several categories, showing in statistical form the 'top tens' for Lancashire:

The Run-Getters

1.	Ernest Tyldesley	34,222
2.	Johnny Tyldesley	31,949
3.	Cyril Washbrook	27,863
4.	Harry Makepeace	25,207
5.	Frank Watson	22,833
6.	Jack Sharp	22,015
7.	Jack Iddon	21,975
8.	Ken Grieves	20,802
9.	Charlie Hallows	20,142
10.	Alan Wharton	17,921

Batting Averages

1.	Ernest Tyldesley	45.20
2.	Clive Lloyd	44.94
3.	Cyril Washbrook	42.15
4.	Eddie Paynter	41.59
5.	Johnny Tyldesley	41.38
6.	Ken Cranston	40.16
7.	Charlie Hallows	39.72
8.	Graeme Fowler*	37.80
9.	Jack Ikin	37.70
10.	Frank Hayes	37.45

* still playing first-class cricket

Most centuries for Lancashire

1.	Ernest Tyldesley	90
2.	Johnny Tyldesley	73
3.	Cyril Washbrook	58
4.	Charlie Hallows	52
5.	Jack Iddon	46
6.	Harry Makepeace	42
7.	David Lloyd	37
8.=	Eddie Paynter	36
	Jack Sharp	36
10.	Winston Place	34

Most Test Appearances

1.	Clive Lloyd (West Indies)	110
2.	Brian Statham (England)	70
3.	Farokh Engineer (India)	46
4.	Cyril Wahbrook (England)	37
5.	Archie MacLaren (England)	35
6.	Johnny Briggs (England)	33
7.	Johnny Tyldesley (England)	31
8.=	Bob Barber (England)	28
	Geoff Pullar (England)	28
10.	Sydney Barnes (England)	27

Highest Individual Scores

1.	Archie MacLaren	424	v. Somerset	1895
2.	Eddie Paynter	322	v. Sussex	1937
3.	Frank Watson	300*	v. Surrey	1928
4.	Johnny Tyldesley	295*	v. Kent	1906
5.	Winston Place	266*	v. Oxford University	1947
6.	Ernest Tyldesley	256*	v. Warwickshire	1930
7.	Cyril Washbrook	251*	v. Surrey	1947
8.	Reg Spooner	247	v. Nottinghamshire	1903
9.	Charlie Hallows	233	v. Hampshire	1927
10.	Graeme Fowler	226	v. Kent	1984

Eddie Paynter also scored	291	v. Hampshire	1938
	226	v. Essex	1937
Johnny Tyldesley scored	272	v. Derbyshire	1919
	253	v. Kent	1914
	250	v. Nottinghamshire	1905
	249	v. Leicestershire	1899
	248	v. Worcestershire	1903
	243	v. Leicestershire	1908
	225	v. Nottinghamshire	1904
Archie MacLaren scored	244	v. Kent	1897
	226*	v. Kent	1896
Frank Watson also scored	236	v. Sussex	1928
Winston Place also scored	226*	v. Nottinghamshire	1949

Ernest Tyldesley scored	244	v.	Warwickshire	1927
	242	v.	Leicestershire	1928
	239	v.	Glamorgan	1934
	236	v.	Surrey	1923
Cyril Washbrook scored	228	v.	Oxford University	1935
Reg Spooner scored	240	v.	Somerset	1906
Charlie Hallows scored	232	v.	Sussex	1928
	227	v.	Warwickshire	1921

Most Wickets

1.	Brian Statham	1,816
2.	Johnny Briggs	1,696
3.	Arthur Mold	1,543
4.	Dick Tyldesdley	1,449
5.	Alec Watson	1,308
6.	Harry Dean	1,267
7.	Roy Tattersall	1,168
8.	Ted McDonald	1,053
9.	Ken Higgs	1,033
10.	Dick Pollard	1,015

Bowling Averages

1.	Alec Watson	13.39
2.	Richard Barlow	13.60
3.	Brian Statham	15.12
4.	Arthur Mold	15.15
5.	Johnny Briggs	15.60
6.	Cecil Parkin	16.12
7.	Dick Tyldesley	16.65
8.	Roy Tattersall	17.39
9.	Harry Dean	18.01
10.	Malcolm Hilton	18.81

Allan Steel actually heads the bowling averages, with 238 wickets at a cost of 3,134, an average of 13.16 but, since he only played 47 matches for Lancashire, I have not included him in this list of Lancashire's Top Tens.

Lancashire Cricketing Greats
Batting Averages
(Up to the end of the 1988 season)

	Matches	Innings	N.O.s	Runs	H. Sc.	Average
Paul Allott	165	183	42	2,480	88	17.58
Bob Barber	155	264	25	6,760	175	28.28
Richard Barlow	249	426	45	7,765	117	20.38
Sydney Barnes	46	58	20	452	35	11.89
Robert Berry	93	85	34	427	27*	8.37
Jack Bond	344	522	76	11,867	157	26.60
Walter Brearley	106	145	23	749	38	6.13
Johnny Briggs	391	602	39	10,707	186	19.01
Ken Cranston	50	57	9	1,928	155*	40.16
Willis Cuttell	213	294	30	5,389	137	20.41
Harry Dean	256	354	118	2,449	49*	10.37
George Duckworth	424	455	170	4,174	75	14.64
Farokh Engineer	175	262	39	5,942	141	26.64
William Farrimond	134	142	38	2,202	63	21.17
Graeme Fowler	159	267	17	9,450	226	37.80
Tommy Greenhough	241	298	79	1,868	76*	8.52
Ken Grieves	452	696	73	20,802	224	33.39
Charlie Hallows	370	569	62	20,142	233*	39.72
Frank Hayes	228	339	48	10,899	187	37.45
Ken Higgs	306	374	131	2,655	60	10.92
Malcolm Hilton	241	294	35	3,140	100*	12.12
Len Hopwood	397	571	54	15,519	220	30.01
Albert Hornby	292	467	28	10,649	188	24.25
Nigel Howard	170	234	29	5,526	145	26.95
David Hughes	389	513	91	2,293	153	22.02
Jack Iddon	483	683	90	21,975	222	37.05
Jack Ikin	288	431	51	14,327	192	37.70
Peter Lever	268	285	59	3,073	83	13.59
Clive Lloyd	219	326	42	12,764	217*	44.94
David Lloyd	378	605	70	17,877	195	33.41
Archie MacLaren	307	510	37	15,772	424	33.34

Harry Makepeace	487	757	64	25,207	203	36.67
Ted McDonald	217	215	31	1,868	100*	10.15
Arthur Mold	260	347	114	1,675	57	7.15
Cecil Parkin	157	189	27	1,959	57	12.09
Eddie Paynter	293	445	47	16,555	322	41.59
Harry Pilling	323	525	65	14,841	149*	32.26
Winston Place	298	441	43	14,605	266*	36.69
Dick Pollard	266	298	52	3,273	63	13.30
Geoff Pullar	312	524	45	16,853	167*	35.18
Vernon Royle	74	120	8	1,754	81	15.66
Jack Sharp	518	776	70	22,015	211	31.18
Ken Shuttleworth	177	179	62	1,929	71	16.48
Jack Simmons	417	517	136	8,681	112	22.78
Reg Spooner	170	280	14	9,889	247	37.17
Brian Statham	430	501	98	4,237	62	10.51
Allan Steel	47	72	5	1,960	105	29.95
Roy Tattersall	277	312	128	1,786	58	9.70
Ernest Tyldesley	573	850	93	34,222	256*	45.20
Johnny Tyldesley	507	824	52	31,949	295*	41.38
Dick Tyldesley	374	435	47	6,126	105	15.78
Albert Ward	330	554	47	15,392	185	30.96
Cyril Washbrook	500	756	95	27,863	251*	42.15
Alec Watson	283	423	88	4,187	74	12.49
Frank Watson	456	664	48	22,833	300*	37.06
Alan Wharton	392	589	55	17,921	199	33.55
Barry Wood	260	424	56	12,969	198	35.42

Bowling averages

(up to the end of the 1988 season)

	Runs	Wickets	Best	Average
Paul Allott	11,079	475	8–48	23.32
Bob Barber	4,768	152	7–35	31.36
Richard Barlow	10,010	736	9–39	13.60
Sydney Barnes	4,459	225	8–37	19.81

Robert Berry	5,900	259	10–102	22.77
Jack Bond	69	0	—	—
Walter Brearley	12,907	690	9–47	18.70
Johnny Briggs	26,464	1,696	10–55	15.60
Ken Cranston	3,267	142	7–43	23.00
Willis Cuttell	14,890	760	8–105	19.59
Harry Dean	22,828.	1,267	9–31	18.01
George Duckworth	66	0	—	—
Farokh Engineer	10	0	—	—
William Farrimond	16	0	—	—
Graeme Fowler	117	5	2–34	23.40
Tommy Greenhough	15,540	707	7–56	21.98
Ken Grieves	6,769	235	6–60	28.80
Charlie Hallows	784	19	3–28	41.26
Frank Hayes	11	0	—	—
Ken Higgs	23,661	1,033	7–19	22.90
Malcolm Hilton	17,419	926	8–19	18.81
Len Hopwood	14,905	672	9–33	22.18
Albert Hornby	94	3	1–2	31.33
Nigel Howard	23	0	—	—
David Hughes	17,505	596	7–24	29.37
Jack Iddon	14,214	533	9–42	26.66
Jack Ilkin	8,005	278	6–21	28.79
Peter Lever	17,647	716	7–70	24.64
Clive Lloyd	1,809	55	4–48	32.89
David Lloyd	7,007	234	7–38	29.94
Archie MacLaren	247	1	1–44	247.00
Harry Makepeace	1,971	42	4–33	46.92
Ted McDonald	22,079	1053	8–53	20.96
Arthur Mold	23,384	1543	9–29	15.15
Cecil Parkin	14,526	901	9–32	16.12
Eddie Paynter	1,250	24	3–13	52.08
Harry Pilling	195	1	1–42	195.00
Winston Place	42	1	1–2	42.00
Dick Pollard	22,492	1,015	8–33	22.15
Geoff Pullar	305	8	3–91	38.12
Vernon Royle	114	2	1–22	57.00
Jack Sharp	11,821	434	9–77	27.23
Ken Shuttleworth	11,097	484	7–41	22.92
Jack Simmons	25,958	974	7–64	26.65
Reg Spooner	554	5	1–5	110.80

Brian Statham	27,470	1,816	8–34	15.12
Allan Steel	3,134	238	9–63	13.16
Roy Tattersall	20,316	1,168	9–40	17.39
Ernest Tyldesley	332	6	3–33	55.33
Johnny Tyldesley	170	2	1–4	85.00
Dick Tyldesley	24,139	1,449	8–15	16.65
Albert Ward	2,380	65	6–29	36.61
Cyril Washbrook	268	4	1–4	67.00
Alec Watson	17,516	1,308	9–118	13.39
Frank Watson	12,811	402	5–31	31.86
Alan Wharton	7,094	225	7–33	31.52
Barry Wood	6,910	251	7–52	27.52

Wicket Keeping

	Caught	Stumped	Total
George Duckworth	634	288	922
Farokh Engineer	429	35	464
William Farrimond	232	65	297